ADVANCE PRAISE

"As a result of a highly successful advisory and consulting career, Ram Charan has studied innumerable companies and their management systems. *The Amazon Management System* challenges readers and their organizations to understand and then implement the management system that shortly will be demanded by their customers."

—Larry Bossidy, former CEO of Honeywell and coauthor of *Execution,* which spent more than 150 weeks on the *New York Times* bestseller list.

"Amazon is secretive, but it is not a black box. The management secrets of this supremely successful company are here, revealed by Ram Charan and Julia Yang. You can't afford not to read this fascinating book."

—Geoff Colvin, bestselling author and Senior Editor-at-Large, *Fortune*

"Ram does it again. He distills the maximum brilliance from a very complex company into the minimum number of pages, leaving the reader smarter and better prepared."

—Johnny C. Taylor, Jr., President & CEO, Society for Human Resource Management (SHRM)

"Most of us watch in awe as Amazon dominates the competition with nonstop rapid-fire disruption. But they are no outlier. Anyone can replicate their success by learning Amazon's management system as revealed in this short but powerful book."

—Charlene Li, bestselling author of *The Disruption Mindset* and Senior Fellow at Altimeter, a Prophet company

"Amazon's incredible success is a premier case study of organization reinvention. Ram and Julia discover and define six building blocks of Amazon's success that can be adapted to any organization. Their easy to read ideas and simple to do actions template are the playbook for anyone wanting to create a more effective organization."

—Dave Ulrich, Rensis Likert Professor, Ross School of Business, University of Michigan coauthor of *Reinventing the Organization*

"No company should try to be like Amazon. But every company can learn from Amazon. Ram Charan and Julia Yang reveal how you can adapt elements from Amazon into your own 21st-century management system to become stronger, smarter, faster, and more successful."

—Thomas A. Stewart, Executive Director, National Center for the Middle Market and co-author of *Woo, Wow, and Win: Service Design, Strategy, and the Art of Customer Delight*

"As I was reading this short, to-the-point book, I paused and reflected about our own management system and determined what I needed to change. Whether it's data, machine learning; cash flow, hiring or customer obsession, Amazon is the leader to learn from and this book is the guide."

—Michael J. Graff, Chairman, CEO and President, American Air Liquide

"[Ram] has the rare ability to distill meaningful from meaningless and transfer it in a quiet, effective way without destroying confidences."

—Jack Welch, former Chairman of GE

"[Ram is my] secret weapon."

—Ivan Seidenberg, former CEO of Verizon

"[Ram]'s like your conscience,"

—John Reed, former CEO of Citicorp

"The most influential consultant alive."

—Fortune Magazine

THE amazon MANAGEMENT SYSTEM

WILEY

THE amazon MANAGEMENT SYSTEM

The Ultimate Digital Business Engine That Creates Extraordinary Value *for* Both Customers *and* Shareholders

RAM CHARAN

Coauthor of EXECUTION *(With Larry Bossidy)*,
A NEW YORK TIMES BESTSELLER

JULIA YANG

The Amazon Management System

Authorized reprint by Wiley India Pvt. Ltd., 4436/7, Ansari Road, Daryaganj, New Delhi - 110002. Under Licence from Ideapress Publishing, USA.

Cover Design by Pete Garceau
Interior Design by Jessica Angerstein

Reprint: 2020

Printed in India by Sanat Printers.

ISBN: 978-81-265-6087-5

From Ram

Dedicated to the hearts and souls of the joint family of twelve siblings and cousins living under one roof for fifty years, whose personal sacrifices made my formal education possible.

From Julia

Dedicated to Judy, my daughter, who continues to amaze, inspire and enlighten me.

OUR PURPOSE

Going forward, all companies will be digital. The century-old management approach designed for command and control has become obsolete.

What's the new way of thinking and managing in the digital age? The Amazon management system and the six building blocks methodically analyzed in this book can be enlightening for all.

Our research is based on public sources, interviews of ex-and current Amazon executives, and cross-checking of facts. Some of the Amazon tools and best practices have been introduced to our clients and have been proven useful and effective.

For you, our dear readers, we are not suggesting that you become Amazon; but that you understand how it works and pick the valuable ingredients and inspirations for your own digital way.

This book will be a short read. If coupled with intense reflections, it will generate relevant, practical, and useful learnings.

CONTENTS

CHAPTER HIGHLIGHTS

WHY THIS BOOK?

WHY NOW?

WHY AMAZON?

WHAT'S THE AMAZON MANAGEMENT SYSTEM?

BUILDING BLOCK 1: Customer-Obsessed Business Model

BUILDING BLOCK 2: Continuous Bar-Raising Talent Pool

BUILDING BLOCK 3: AI-Powered Data & Metrics System

BUILDING BLOCK 4: Ground-Breaking Invention Machine

BUILDING BLOCK 5: High-Velocity & High-Quality Decision-Making

BUILDING BLOCK 6: Forever-Day-1 Culture

WHY DOES THIS MATTER TO YOU, AND EVERYONE?

Founders and business owners

Senior executives

Junior to middle managers

The young and fresh

The entrepreneurs

WHY THIS BOOK?

WHY NOW?

Our 21st century prevailing management systems are still largely inherited from the oldest forms of human organization, such as the military and the church. They were designed for the purpose of command and control in an age when there was no Internet, no smartphone, and none of the various forms of digital technology such as big data, algorithms and AI, and when personal supervision was the only way to keep an eye on employees.

The military and the church were organized by function and had many hierarchical layers. So were the business organizations that mimicked their management system.

Then there came an important innovation: Pierre DuPont of the DuPont Corporation and Alfred Sloan of General Motors created divisional structure in the 1920s. Then the matrix structure evolved in the 1960s to accommodate the global market and global supply chain. However, as businesses grew bigger, the number of layers went up, bureaucracy increased, and decision making slowed down.

In the 1980s Jack Welch of GE created the concept of the operating system. While the intensity of execution increased, the number of layers remained large, bureaucracy remained intense, decision-making remained slow, and the chain between manufacturers and end-users remained long.

Moreover, such a management system was not focused on customers or on innovating for customers. Instead, organizational leaders fixated on competition with a mindset deeply entrenched in achieving incremental growth slightly better than GDP, gaining market share against a few key competitors, and benchmarking best practices here and there.

This old management approach has become obsolete in the digital age. Amazon is one of the biggest reasons why.

WHY AMAZON?

The arrival of the digital pioneers, such as Amazon's founder and CEO Jeff Bezos, disrupted these corporate leadership models of the past. No one is more determined than Amazon to reinvent the management system by using tools that have become available in the digital era.

The Amazon management system is truly revolutionary. It delivers a superb end-to-end customer experience that is better, cheaper, faster, and more convenient; it drives continuous inventions on behalf of customers; it creates new businesses, expands the eco-system and more importantly, increases cash flows from gross margin that have enabled continuous investment in technology infrastructure and innovation. It not only creates tremendous value for customers, but also creates the world's best value for shareholders.

Legendary investor Warren Buffett, in an interview with *CNN*, called Amazon a "miracle."

Amazon market value in US Dollars

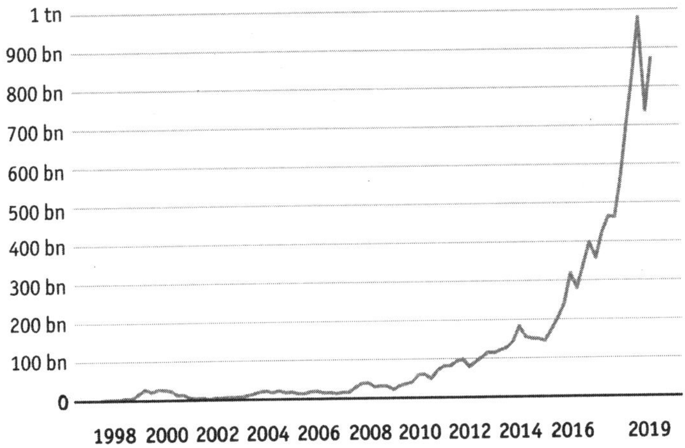

Source: Bloomberg

Amazon revenue in US Dollars

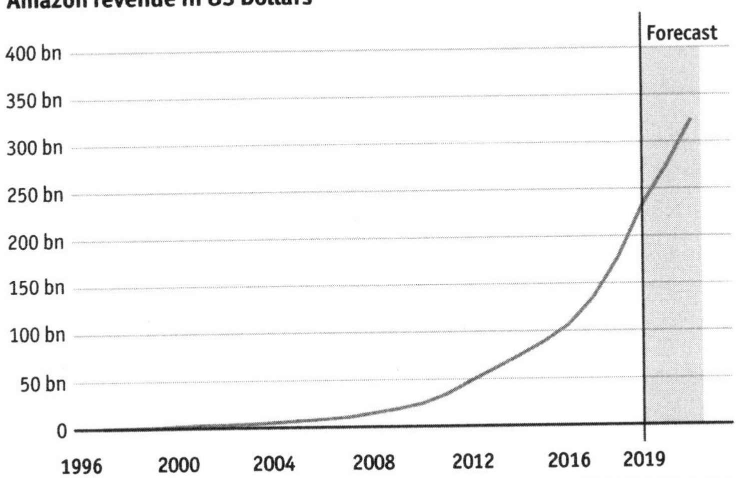

Source: Bloomberg

WHAT IS THE AMAZON MANAGEMENT SYSTEM?

At the heart of all Amazon's business endeavors is the Amazon management system, a digital engine composed of six building blocks, that has been continuously and relentlessly empowering Amazon for more growth and more exploration into the unlimited sky of the digital age.

The Amazon management system breaks new ground in the following ways:

BUILDING BLOCK 1: CUSTOMER-OBSESSED BUSINESS MODEL

Despite their espoused commitment to putting the customer first, most traditional companies operate quite differently: they tend to be competition centric. They pay a huge amount of attention to financial results, especially earnings per share, and dance to the quarter-by-quarter short-term rhythm set by the capital market.

Amazon's business model, on the contrary, is customer-obsessed, continuously expanding, built on novel concepts of platform, ecosystem and infrastructure, able to defy traditional laws of diminishing returns, and actually delivers increasing cash flows and higher return on investment.

BUILDING BLOCK 2: CONTINUOUS BAR-RAISING TALENT POOL

Most traditional companies spend enormous amounts of money and effort in recruiting, developing, and retaining talent, and yet still encounter huge difficulty in finding the right people and deploying them in the right jobs. Take recruiting for example, many companies lack specific standards, and even if there are standards, they will easily give way to the pressing business urgency.

Amazon's talent pool is carefully defined, meticulously documented, and rigorously chosen; and coupled with complete end-to-end follow-through and feedback to ensure continuous bar-raising, both for the talent pool itself and for the self-reinforcing mechanism of talent acquisition and retention.

In all interviews, Amazon includes a designated and trained person known as the "bar-raiser." They ensure that the hire is a fit for Amazon's culture and its continuous bar-raising.

BUILDING BLOCK 3: AI-POWERED DATA AND METRICS SYSTEM

In most companies founded pre-digital, data is scattered and fragmented within different silos, layers, and business units producing significant latency of weeks and months. People seeking a full picture of what is really happening in any day-to-day operation must spend intensive efforts involving many people, and suffer long wait times, in order to dig beneath the results on the surface.

Many of you can remember the painful experience and mounting frustrations of trying to gather important information from various divisions to piece together a complete picture for you, your team, or a presentation. In some companies, this need alone could justify a big division.

In such a setup, monthly or quarterly reviews could easily last hours or even days, as business and functional leaders sort through their pieces of the jigsaw puzzle one by one; then such work spirals out of control when the business grows bigger, the number of employees increases, and layers are added, due to the limitation of time and energy of any human being, i.e., the rule of "spanof control."

Amazon leverages modern technology to run day-to-day operations differently. Amazon's data and metrics system is ultra-detailed, cross-silo, cross-layer, end-to-end, real-time, input-oriented and AI-powered; therefore everything can be tracked, measured, and analyzed in real time with anomaly detected, insights generated, and routine decisions automated.

In this way, it provides a single source of truth and significantly minimizes the need for "personal supervision," thus enabling massive reduction in organizational layers.

BUILDING BLOCK 4:
GROUND-BREAKING INVENTION MACHINE

Most companies began before Amazon build their success on one brilliant innovation they made a long time ago. After that super-lucky and destiny-defining moment, many shy away from ground-breaking inventions, and seem complacent with minor improvements afterwards, here and there, year after year, and sometimes limited to only the packaging.

On this front, Amazon has surprised us all. Amazon's invention machine is continuous, accelerating, and aimed at generating ground-breaking, game-changing, and customer behavior-shaping inventions that create new market spaces and economic opportunities of massive magnitude.

BUILDING BLOCK 5:
HIGH-VELOCITY AND HIGH-QUALITY DECISION-MAKING

Another systematic flaw with legacy management systems: decision-making happens at what feels like a glacial pace, with a "one-size-fits-all" approach applied to almost all matters requiring a yes or no. All kinds of frustrations litter a typically lengthy approval process composed of numerous executives and committees and decision are further stalled by all kinds of politics, backstabbing, gaming-the-system, and the routine charades of maximizing requests on resources, and minimizing commitments on results. All of us are probably familiar with this from own experiences.

Amazon's decision-making is high-quality, high-velocity, and strictly follows a set of clearly articulated principles and uniquely designed toolsets enforced with striking consistency throughout the organization. This can make the company a very demanding place to work, but it frees employees from many of the headaches mentioned above.

BUILDING BLOCK 6:
FOREVER-DAY-1 CULTURE

As they get bigger, most legacy companies find they have long lost the initial speed, agility, and vitality commonly found in start-ups. They have become rigid, slow, and risk-averse; complacency and bureaucracy have crept in. Some could sustain for a while, some would gradually fall into oblivion or irrelevance, some would become the prey for aggressive acquirers, and only a few could continuously refresh themselves.

Amazon, as an organization, is committed to be forever Day 1, that is, to combine the size and scale advantages of a big company, the speed and agility of a startup, and the continuous upgrade of organizational capabilities.

WHY DOES THIS MATTER TO YOU, AND EVERYONE?

Make no mistake. Every leader, every entrepreneur, every manager, and every employee, with no exception, must recognize that the century-old management system has become obsolete, and that to survive and thrive in the digital age, all companies need to learn and find a new way that best fits them.

IT'S A MUST, NOT OPTIONAL.

FOUNDERS AND BUSINESS OWNERS

Going forward, all companies will be digital. Every company will have a platform of its own and/or be connected to someone else's platform.

Old companies, even old industries, could be disrupted and destroyed; new market spaces and enormous economic opportunities are being created at the same time. The digital giants are the driving forces behind many major changes in the digital age.

The good news is that most of your legacy peers have not started down this path yet, so if you get a head start on embarking on the digitization journey, you may improve your chances to take the lead.

The choice is yours to make: to die or to digitize and achieve exponential value creation.

SENIOR EXECUTIVES

In the digital age, your job content will change radically.

Instead of spending most of your time supervising others and attending endless reviews, meetings, and committees, your job will be to study consumers directly (not through filters) and drive continuous innovation for them. Your job will require learning how to manage day-to-day operations by using data and metrics with digital tools, to hone your judgment, to make high-leverage decisions, to create mission-critical cross-functional teams with clear goals and specific outputs that innovate and deliver a better user experience, as well as to allocate resources and make mid-course adjustment in a timely fashion.

You will need to be imaginative, to be able to reinvent the business, organization and management system using digital tools, and to lead the transformation. Otherwise, digitization could be a big disruptor for you; and perhaps .... the terminator.

JUNIOR TO MIDDLE MANAGERS

As more companies make the transition to the kinds of Amazon management practices described here, leaders will remove management layers, requiring you to reimagine your job and rebuild your competence. Just as the management reforms of the 1980s and 1990s "re-engineered" corporations and removed redundant roles, the digital age is doing this again through the filter of data analysis.

We expect to see reductions in corporate multilayer structures from seven, nine, or twelve layers to no more than five, four, or even three layers. This will reduce the traditional management pool by as much as eight in ten.

This change is inevitable. We have worked with large traditional companies that have gone from eight layers to three layers, and quickly become disruptors to their traditional and digital competitors.

Don't be disheartened: this in fact presents you with an opportunity. You can go with the wind and take advantage of it, becoming more prosperous, more satisfied, and achieving faster personal growth. You can benefit by understanding the digital management system, proactively preparing yourself in mindset and skill set, and becoming a catalyst instead of a roadblock in the coming management digitization.

THE YOUNG AND FRESH

There has never been a better era for new talent — the young and fresh.

The more you understand the Amazon management system, the more contributions you can make, and the more successful you will be in your career whether you are working for a company or starting your own.

Most companies (by most we mean 99%), whether digital or traditional, are looking for young talent who are hard-working, eager to learn, and demonstrate the necessary aptitude, mindset, and skill set required in the new system. Many of them are willing (indeed, forced) to promote these high-potential young people faster and take a risk on their inexperience.

So it's your time to shine now. Learn fast and get ready.

THE ENTREPRENEURS

For your start-ups, please stop copying the management system from GE or other industrial-age companies. Do not follow the traditional 100-year-old wisdom.

Eschew seven or more layers, avoid silo-based organization structure, and choose superior alternatives to the once-a-year annual strategy, budget, KPI, and evaluation processes. Trust and apply the digital way.

Learn from the digital giants and the relentless inventors, such as Amazon, whose management system has been systematically described in this book. All the elements that have fueled Amazon's tremendous success create unparalleled opportunities for you to start building the superstars of tomorrow. Leveraging a digital management system will help your start-ups scale much faster than ever — far beyond traditional expectations.

Find a new way to get the most from the digital age and experiment with what works best for you.

* * * * * * * *

In many ways, Amazon has defied the traditional laws of business operation and the core building blocks of the Amazon management system have demonstrated a new formula for winning in the digital age.

Again we are not here to advocate a blind replication of all and everything in the Amazon management system. We hope that this book can help you understand how it works and pick the valuable ingredients and inspirations for your own digital way.

As you read our book, you will see we have focused on the positive aspects of what Amazon does right and what you can learn from that. The brand has been in the news recently and featured in critical articles about everything from environmental impact to labor practices. Many of these are serious issues and warrant serious consideration and action. Amazon's clout and visibility makes its decisions in these areas even more worthy of attention. In this book, we will not be addressing those concerns directly — but rather looking specifically from a management perspective and what you can learn about Amazon's model for creating value and the six building blocks you can apply to your own business.

CHAPTER HIGHLIGHTS

BUILDING BLOCK 1

Amazon's business model is customer-obsessed, continuously expanding, built on novel concepts of platform, ecosystem, infrastructure and personalization (M=1), able to defy traditional laws of diminishing returns, and actually delivers increasing cash flows and higher return on investment.

WHAT'S AMAZON BUSINESS MODEL?

1.0: Online bookstore

2.0: Online everything store

3.0: Unstore - online platform

4.0: Infrastructure and online and offline platform

WHAT'S ITS UNDERLYING LOGIC?

Customer obsession

Relentless drive to invent

Long-term thinking

Earnings vs. cash generation

HOW TO MAKE IT WORK?

BUILDING BLOCK 1:

CUSTOMER-OBSESSED BUSINESS MODEL

Before starting Amazon, Jeff Bezos worked at D. E. Shaw and Co., a Wall Street firm famous for its quantitative trading methods. In 1994, founder David Shaw appointed Bezos to lead the effort to study potential business opportunities that could be created by the Internet. The two would spend a few hours brainstorming each week, and Bezos would conduct further study to explore the feasibility of their ideas.

Among those seemingly crazy ideas generated twenty-five years ago, some indeed came true, such as the "concept of a free, advertising-supported email service for consumers – the idea behind Gmail and Yahoo Mail," "a new kind of financial service that allowed Internet users to trade stocks and bonds online" – the idea behind E-Trade, and last but not the least, "the everything store."[1]

When Bezos studied the Internet, a magic number caught his attention: **2300%**. Web activity had increased by a factor of roughly 2300% in the past year. Bezos noted, "It's highly unusual, and that started me thinking, what kind of business plan might make sense in the context of that growth?"[2] With this notion in mind, he decided to quit his lucrative, highly promising career on Wall Street and start his own business.

Twenty-five years ago, the Internet was still in its infancy. So where should Bezos start? How to conceptualize a dynamic business model with unlimited growth that had both the high potential to ride this wave of unprecedented growth and the solid feasibility to convert his ambition into reality?

WHAT'S AMAZON'S BUSINESS MODEL?

Although extremely excited by the unprecedented growth, Bezos sensibly realized that it was highly impractical to launch the "everything store" right from the beginning.

So where to start? Bezos listed twenty product categories that had potential to sell online, such as computer software, office supplies, apparel, and music. After careful contemplation, he decided that the best starting point should be books.

1.0: ONLINE BOOKSTORE

Why books?

You can probably come up with several obvious reasons yourself. Books are highly standardized, the market is big, and the logistics of shipping books is relatively less challenging than shipping other things.

The less obvious reason is that at that time the book market was heavily dominated by only two distributors. For a start-up, it was much easier to deal with two, rather than thousands, if not hundreds of thousands, suppliers at the same time.

But the most important reason was that the Internet could provide enormous competitive edges in the book game.

Why? Back then, a typical bookstore would carry 100,000 books in stock, only a fraction of the roughly 3 million titles in print. All physical bookstores were constrained by a practical ceiling of how many books they could carry, while an online bookstore could offer an "unlimited selection".

This was exactly the crucial differentiator that Bezos had been looking for to feed his game-changing ambition. He understood that the Internet would change customers' shopping experience in a fundamental way. So what other magic tricks could the budding Internet do?

There were two more worth noting. One is customer reviews. Unlike the flattering reviews by famous figures included on physical books as part of marketing efforts, reviews on the Internet would come from ordinary readers, direct, authentic and unfiltered. The unlimited space on the web meant that all reviews, positive or negative, could be shown in their entirety, as posted.

The other is personalization. Bezos envisioned that one day they could achieve the ultimate in personalization: a different version of the website for each customer based on the patterns and preferences derived from his or her previous shopping records. This would be a whole new experience for customers, made possible only on the emerging Internet.

With "unlimited selection," "unfiltered customer reviews," and "ultimate personalization," the three unmatchable and innate advantages of the Internet, Bezos was confident that no physical bookstores, no matter how big they were then, could be serious competitors in the long run.

That's perhaps why the word "Amazon" instantly enchanted Bezos when he tried to find a good name for his start-up. He had experimented with names such as Awake.com, Browse.com, Bookmall.com, Relentless.com, Makeitso.com, as well as Cadabra. Still searching, Bezos referred to the dictionary. Luckily the name hunt didn't last long. Amazon jumped out at him. It was love at first sight. Amazon "is not only the largest river in the world. It's many times larger than the next biggest river. It blows all other rivers away," Bezos said.

Yes, Amazon, it was.

The name spoke to Bezos's dramatic ambition at the time. His goal was to build an online bookstore that would not only be the largest in the whole world, but could also blow all other bookstores away.

Clearly Bezos achieved his goal. Amazon has become **the indisputable leader in the book market**. In 2018 in the US, it commanded a dominating share of 42% in physical books and a staggering share of 89% in E-books (as shown below).

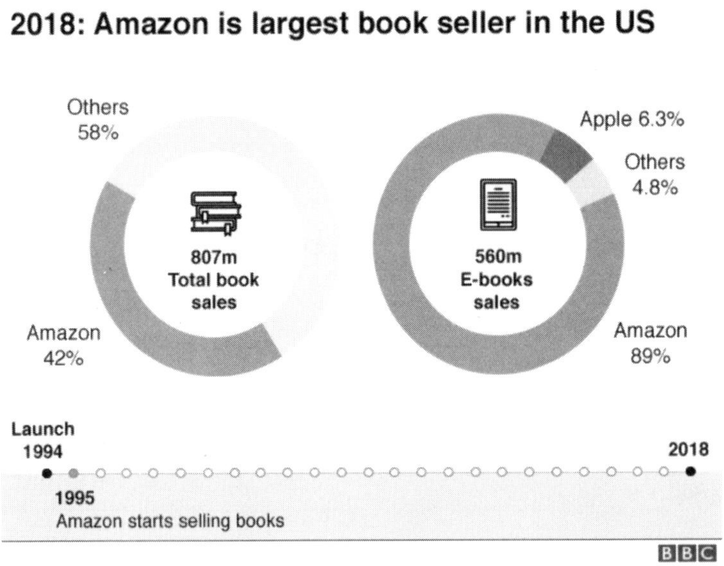

2.0: ONLINE EVERYTHING STORE

Despite Amazon's burgeoning book business, Bezos never forgot his dream of "the everything store." In 1998, Amazon started its first wave of expansions into new categories such as music, video, and gifts; and into new geographies, such as the UK and Germany. After that, the company accelerated its further expansions into toys, consumer electronics, home improvement, software, video games, and many more. This was the kernel of Bezos's vision.

While enjoying dramatic organic growth in these earlier categories, Amazon also made numerous investments and acquisitions, such as Drugstore.com, Pets Smart, Accept.com, HomeGrocer.com, Gear.com, Back to Basics Toys, Greenlight.com (online car retailer), Wine Shopper.com, Audible.de, Zappos, and many others.[3] Despite the variety, you can discern a common underlying theme.

At a dazzling speed, Amazon had woven together a magnificent tapestry of the everything store.

During this time of rapid growth of categories, geographies, and acquisitions, Bezos kept his laser-sharp focus on the customer. In 2001 he articulated Amazon's "pillars of customer experiences" for the first time and reinforced the durability of these pillars in his 2008 Shareholder Letter:

1. Selection: already 45,000 items and millions of book titles on sale in 2001.
2. Convenience: a combination of 1-click ordering, recommendations, wish lists, instant order update, "Look Inside the Book" and fast delivery.
3. Low price: not simply by the scale of economy, but more so by the Moore's Law and its variants (price performance of bandwidth, disk space and processing power are doubling about every 9, 12, and 18 months, respectively).

Why this constant focus on the customers? Because Bezos firmly believes that "our consumer franchise is our most valuable asset."

Amazon launched Prime in 2005, a $79 annual membership fee for free two-day shipping. As of December 31, 2018, Amazon had more than 100M prime members around the world, the second-highest number of paid subscribers only next to Netflix.[4]

Interestingly, the principle of focusing on the customer will result in the best creation of shareholder value.

3.0: UNSTORE — ONLINE PLATFORM

What's a platform and how is it different from a store?

A first party selling business is a store, and would not qualify as a platform. A platform engages multiple parties, facilitates complicated transactions and/or interactions with multiple products and services, and creates value for all parties involved.

To have Amazon truly become a platform, Bezos coined the concept of the "unstore," in order to reframe the notion of Amazon to those who saw it as merely a retailer that had set up shop in a digital zip code. He repeatedly explained and elaborated on why Amazon is a technology company, not a retailer. He argued that Amazon should only concern itself with what is best for the customers, helping them to make the best choices.

This decision would have enormous operational and strategic implications. Amazon would not be bound by traditional retail rules, and, more importantly, would center its efforts on how to build long-term trust-based relationships with customers, instead of how to maximize short-term revenue and profits through its first-party sales.

That's why after two failed attempts to attract third-party sellers (both launched in 1999, Amazon Auctions abandoned in 2000, and ZShops abandoned in 2007), Amazon audaciously launched the Marketplace, an e-commerce platform owned and operated by Amazon that enables third-party sellers to sell new or used products alongside Amazon's regular offerings.

In the beginning, many people were baffled by Amazon's decision to list search results of items from first-party and third-party sellers on the same page, to empower third-party sellers with all kinds of powerful analytical and management tools, and even to share with them Amazon's own customer base and core competencies, such as fulfillment.

To anyone who would view Amazon's business model as an online store, its generous offerings to third-party sellers seemed totally insane. Why help your competitors? And yet, to anyone who sees Amazon as a platform, the choice totally makes sense. Because in the platform model, third-party sellers are not competitors, but valuable ecosystem partners. Amazon has built an ecosystem of millions of small and medium-sized businesses, third-party sellers, developers, delivery service providers and authors.[5]

By oneself alone, one can never build a platform; by working together with ecosystem partners, a platform will emerge, develop and gradually flourish with a booming ecosystem attached. That's one of the critical new laws of the game in the digital age. Amazon had the prescience to recognize the dynamic business models increasingly possible under the laws of the digital economy; and created unimaginable value by having these insights early enough to act on them boldly and accelerate the benefits of their interrelated aspects.

Amazon's famous flywheel (shown below) visually and vividly illustrates the inner logic of how a platform works.

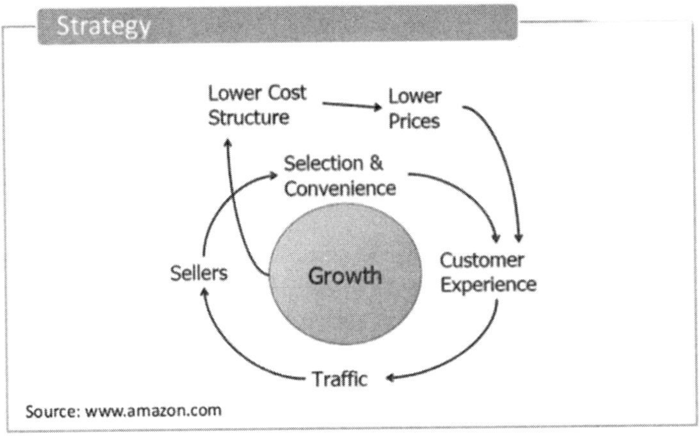

As a standalone online store, one can offer only so many items and serve so many customers, and essentially grow in a linear manner. The platform business model opens everything up for third-party sellers, who trigger growth of a higher order—a jump from linear to exponential, Newtonian to quantum.

More sellers will bring in more selection, attract more customers (i.e., traffic), and thus increase scale (i.e., growth). Increased scale will further reduce cost structure, and will translate into even lower prices for the customers. With increase in selection, decrease in price and likely improvement of convenience (another side benefit of increased scale), the customer experience will be enhanced. The enhanced customer experience will generate more traffic, thus further driving the growth of a powerful flywheel.

This is exactly the innate beauty of platform. All Amazon's generous offerings to and strong empowerment of third-party sellers, its partners within the ecosystem, are the self-reinforcing mechanism for the long-term growth and prosperity of Amazon's platform.

By 2018, Amazon had become the biggest online sales platform with 45% share in the US (as shown below). Third-party selling achieved a staggering 52% compound annual sales growth rate, and grew from

$0.1Bn in 1999 to $160Bn in 2018.[6] Bezos joked in the 2018 Letter to Shareholders, "The percentages represent the share of physical gross merchandise sales sold on Amazon by independent third-party sellers – mostly small- and medium-sized businesses – as opposed to Amazon retail's own first party sales. Third-party sales have grown from 3% of the total to 58%. To put it bluntly: Third-party sellers are kicking our first party butt. Badly."

4.0: INFRASTRUCTURE AND ONLINE AND OFFLINE PLATFORM

With the $13.7 billion acquisition of Whole Foods in 2017 and the opening of Amazon Go, Amazon expanded its empire into fresh grocery and offline. Actually Amazon had been experimenting with the fresh grocery business for several years before the acquisition.

Why was this particular category so important to Amazon? Because shopping for fresh grocery is a high-frequency activity. For some, it may be once a week; for some, it may be two to three times a week; for others, it could be a daily routine. This schedule of **frequent interactions with consumers** is a dream come true for Amazon, a platform that has almost everything for almost everyone. In addition,

Amazon was uniquely positioned to leverage its vast existing customer base, coupled with its unique fulfillment capabilities, to expand into this adjacent space both online and offline.

The most prominent and also most surprising aspect of Amazon's business model is probably its success in infrastructure business, such as Fulfillment By Amazon (FBA, 2006), Amazon Web Services (AWS, 2006), and Alexa (2014).

Despite strong competitive pressure from Microsoft, Google, and Alibaba, AWS remains number one in the global cloud service market with over 40% market share worldwide. In 2018, AWS had millions of customers, ranging from startups to large enterprises, and from government entities to nonprofits,[7] and achieved $26.7 billion revenue, 11% of Amazon's total, and $7.3 billion operating income, 59% of Amazon's total.[8]

How could Amazon make such a successful expansion into infrastructure business?

Over the years, to keep its first party selling business up and running, Amazon has accumulated tremendous expertise in fulfilment and technology. By the traditional theory of competition, companies should safeguard these core competencies as proprietary know-how, strictly using them for internal purposes only. Amazon recognized the new laws of the game in the digital age, and saw how these competitive strengths could open the door to a new option: making it a service to serve external partners.

For example, through FBA, items sold by third-party sellers would be covered under the Prime program, meaning they would quality for two-day free shipping, thus giving a significant boost to their business.

The same line of thought also applies to AWS. These flexible, affordable, convenient, and empowering services are essential for start-ups and SMEs (small to medium enterprises). With cloud services, these companies do not have to make a heavy upfront investment in building their own IT system. Instead they can rely on AWS and simply pay for usage. In this way, Amazon lowered the resources and expertise required to start and grow a business.

Alexa is even more so. It's a cloud- and voice-based AI assistant. In addition to Echo, it is also open to both other companies that create smart devices, and external developers. As Bezos proudly announced:

> *"Since that first-generation Echo, customers have purchased more than 100 million Alexa-enabled devices.... The number of devices with Alexa built-in more than doubled in 2018. There are now more than 150 different products available with Alexa built-in, from headphones and PCs to cars and smart home devices. Much more to come!"*[9]

In this sense, Amazon has become the enabling infrastructure provider for all types of enterprises in the digital age.

Here's another fascinating example of Amazon enabling and anticipating customer needs despite traditional views of competition. As this book was going to press, Amazon announced on September 24, 2019 that it was joining 30 different companies in the "Voice Interoperability Initiative" to ensure as many devices as possible will work with digital assistants from different companies. Amazon is pulling together with its competitors to create an industry standard for voice assistant software and hardware. Notably, Google, Apple, and Samsung are so far sitting out the initiative.

"As much as people would like the headline that there's going to be one voice assistant that rules them all, we don't agree," says Amazon's SVP of devices and services Dave Limp in *The Verge*. "This isn't a sporting event. There's not going to be one winner."

"The initiative is built around a shared belief that voice services should work seamlessly alongside one another on a single device, and that voice-enabled products should be designed to support multiple simultaneous wake words," Amazon reported in its press release. "More than 30 companies are supporting the effort, including global brands like Amazon, Baidu, BMW, Bose, Cerence, ecobee, Harman, Logitech, Microsoft, Salesforce, Sonos, Sound United, Sony Audio Group, Spotify and Tencent; telecommunications operators like Free, Orange, SFR and Verizon; hardware solutions providers like Amlogic,

InnoMedia, Intel, MediaTek, NXP Semiconductors, Qualcomm Technologies, Inc., SGW Global and Tonly; and systems integrators like CommScope, DiscVision, Libre, Linkplay, MyBox, Sagemcom, StreamUnlimited and Sugr.

'Multiple simultaneous wake words provide the best option for customers,' said Jeff Bezos, Amazon founder and CEO. "Utterance by utterance, customers can choose which voice service will best support a particular interaction. It's exciting to see these companies come together in pursuit of that vision.'"

This is another way that throughout twenty-five years of continuous evolution, Amazon has not only grown dramatically in size, but also evolved from simple models and services to far more extensive and dynamic offerings. It has transformed itself from a consumer-facing online bookstore into a consumer-facing platform, both online and offline, both first-party and third-party, for almost everything needed in people's lives—we have yet to see Amazon launch a dating app, but your never know what's coming up!—and into an enterprise-facing enabling infrastructure provider, for logistics and technical services for now, and there is definitely more to come. Amazon's sky is limitless along its multi-dimensional growth trajectory — now and even more so in the future.

Now you see that Amazon has indeed successfully conceived and constructed a continuously expanding business model, built on novel concepts of platform, ecosystem, and infrastructure in the digital age.

WHAT'S AMAZON'S CENTRAL IDEA?

By 2019 Amazon has become a digital giant beyond most people's wildest imagination. In a recent interview with *CNBC*, Charlie Munger, Warren Buffet's right-hand man and decades-long partner, described Amazon as "a phenomenon of nature."

The central idea of Amazon is to imagine a new customer experience that could become a very large market space and an enormous economic opportunity, and imagine a new way to provide and personalize this end-to-end experience through the use of a digital platform and construction of digital infrastructure that processes data via algorithms and orchestrates physical distribution by partners within the ecosystem.

CUSTOMER OBSESSION

Bezos has rarely finished a speech or an interview about Amazon without talking about customer obsession or customer centricity. The first principle that he stated in his famous nine-point management and decision-making approach published in his first Shareholder Letter in 1997 said, "We will continue to focus relentlessly on our customers." Among all 14 Leadership Principles, Customer Obsession, again, ranked number 1, and has remained at the top ever since.

Why has Bezos been so obsessed with the customers?

As noted earlier, he has always regarded customers as Amazon's most valuable asset. Customers are the central piece in Amazon's flywheel and in the entire Amazon platform. Why is Amazon able to aggressively and successfully expand into more and more categories? Because they have customers who would like to buy more. Why are third-party sellers be attracted to the Amazon platform? One of the most obvious reasons is that there are hundreds of millions of customers and, by leveraging Amazon platform, they can scale up much faster.

Despite booming business and growing customer franchise worldwide, Bezos has always remained constantly in **awe of customers**.

> *"There is no rest for the weary. I constantly remind our employees to be afraid, to wake up every morning terrified. Not of our competition, but of our customers. Our customers have made our business what it is, they are the ones with whom we have a relationship, and they are the ones to whom we owe a great obligation. And we consider them to be loyal to us – right up until the second that someone else offers them a better service."*[10]

Customers' trust is an earned privilege, not a long-term benefit to be taken for granted. Trust takes years to build, seconds to break, and forever to repair. That's probably why Bezos emphasized, "Our pricing objective is to earn customer trust, not to optimize short-term profit dollars."[11]

As one of the most (most likely the most) customer-obsessed companies on the planet, Amazon beat out Google and Apple for the top on World's 500 Most Influential Brands list released by World Brand Lab in 2018.

INVENT FOR THE CUSTOMERS

As Bezos put it, "One thing I love about customers is that they are divinely discontent. Their expectations are never static – they go up. It's human nature."[12]

How do we not just meet but stay ahead of the customers' ever-rising expectations? The only way to do this is through continuous innovation and relentless invention. In this way, the divinely discontent customers became the sources of continuous inspiration for Amazon's invention machine.

Many traditional companies also pay serious attention to innovation and improvement, but they normally do so because of competitive or performance pressure. They may seek marginal iterations around the edges, trying to tweak here and there, especially the packaging, but rarely make systematic overhauls for completely new ideas.

What Amazon aspires to is way beyond such minor innovation. At Amazon, the relentless drive to invent dramatic new ways to delight customers never stops. They focus on very big, potentially global consumer needs by visualizing the ultimate inevitability of customer needs, things that will not change in the next ten years (price, selection, and convenience).

Unlike traditional companies that primarily use technology for cost reduction, Amazon focuses on using technology to totally transform the existing customer existing experience, and to imagine an experience that does not exist today, and invent on behalf of the customers, such as Amazon Go.

Take Kindle as another example. It was never meant to out-book the book; it was designed instead to have new capabilities impossible with the traditional book, such as having millions of titles on sale, finding a book and having it in 60 seconds, being able to underline passages and create notes and saving them in the cloud.

In the spirit of relentless drive to invent, Amazon single-handedly created entirely new markets with huge global potential, such as cloud services (AWS) and smart speakers (Echo). As Bezos pointed out:

> *"No one asked for AWS. No one. Turns out the world was in fact ready and hungry for an offering like AWS but didn't know it. We had a hunch, followed our curiosity, took the necessary financial risks, and began building – reworking, experimenting, and iterating countless times as we proceeded."*[13]

LONG-TERM THINKING

"It's all about the long term," noted Bezos in his first Shareholder Letter, adding, "a fundamental measure of our success will be the shareholder value we create over the long term." He went on to say that Amazon "will continue to make investment decisions in light of long-term market leadership considerations rather than short-term profitability considerations or short-term Wall Street reactions."

Why is long-term thinking so important for Amazon? The secret is in the very nature of its business model. Amazon is all about platform and infrastructure. So it is, in essence, a scale business characterized by high fixed costs and relatively low variable costs.

Building platform and infrastructure takes multiple years, and requires massive investments of billions or dozens of billions, if not more. From a short-term perspective, be it quarterly, annually or a two to three-year timeframe, such investments will never be able to generate enough return to cover the initial investments, not to mention generating return. Only those who can think at least seven to ten years out, are able to fully recognize the innate beauty of the platform and infrastructure business: the flywheel, the self-reinforcing mechanism and the exponential growth tilted towards the long term, and thus have the mighty daring to make such massive investments over the long term.

So how to drive the return on such a massive investment? Scale and speed really matter here. Bezos's Letters to Shareholders up to the time of this writing constantly reinforce this philosophy.

First is scale. Increasing scale "spreads fixed costs across more sales, reducing cost per unit, which makes possible more price reductions."[14] Once the scale passes a certain threshold, what Bezos calls the "tipping point," it "allows us to launch new ecommerce businesses faster, with a higher quality of customer experience, a lower incremental cost, a higher chance of success, and a faster path to scale and profitability than any other company."[15]

That's why in 1997, in his first Shareholder Letter, Bezos stated "We will balance our focus on growth with emphasis on long-term profitability and capital management. At this stage, we choose to prioritize growth because we believe that scale is central to achieving the potential of our business model."

Second is speed. Platform and infrastructure are a technology game. Prior investments and faster movements captivate a larger customer base earlier, and accumulate historical data earlier, which translates into significant first-mover advantages in data analytics, algorithm enhancements and AI-driven solutions. In short, all these elements combined create Amazon's **digital core competencies.**

Data is the new equity in the digital age. From customers' data and behavioral analysis, new needs can be identified, better services and experiences can be created and thus more revenue streams can be generated, which further expands the scale, lowers the cost, and increases the return. In fact, each platform must have multiple streams of revenue; otherwise it will never make big money.

Because of its digital core competency, Amazon can continuously improve its operational efficiency while lowering its cost structure, becoming ever more competitive in serving millions more customers.

Such faster iterations of continuous improvements create steep, and increasingly higher, entry barriers for latecomers.

That's why Bezos constantly reminds his team of the importance of velocity, for example emphasizing "greater capital velocity" in the 1997 Shareholder Letter. As the incremental cost of serving more customers converges to almost zero, it's no wonder that Amazon can totally defy the law of diminishing returns,[16] and demonstrate the new law of increasing returns and decreasing incremental costs.

EARNINGS VS. CASH GENERATION

Many people have been baffled by Amazon, which has long been on the verge of barely breakeven, but has enjoyed an unbelievable leap forward in terms of market valuation.

Those who assumed that Amazon is unprofitable or makes little profits are unequivocally mistaken, because the most relevant metric in the digital age is cash earnings per share, not EPS (earnings per share). Unlike the fixed asset investment by traditional companies that can be categorized as CapEx (capital expenditure), and thus depreciated over a multi-year timeframe, many of the investments into the digital tools, systems, and platforms can only be categorized as OpEx (operational expenditure), and thus listed as expenses of the current year, thus lowering the net earnings. Such investments are essential to achieve 25% per year growth.

Amazon's track record disproves this misunderstanding and removes every single shred of delusion that those digital giants will falter because they are not making money in terms of net income. When they achieve appropriate scale, these companies are massive cash machines, making enormous cash.

Why this focus on cash flows, especially gross margin cash generation? As a Wall Street veteran, Bezos fully understands that "a share of stock is a share of a company's future cash flows, and, as a result, cash flows more than any other single variable seem to do the best job of explaining a company's stock price over the long term."[17]

Bezos has walked the talk. And indeed the capital market has rewarded him, in a generous and righteous way.

Amazon 2011-2018 Revenue, gross profits , net cash from operations and net income (Unit: $Bn)

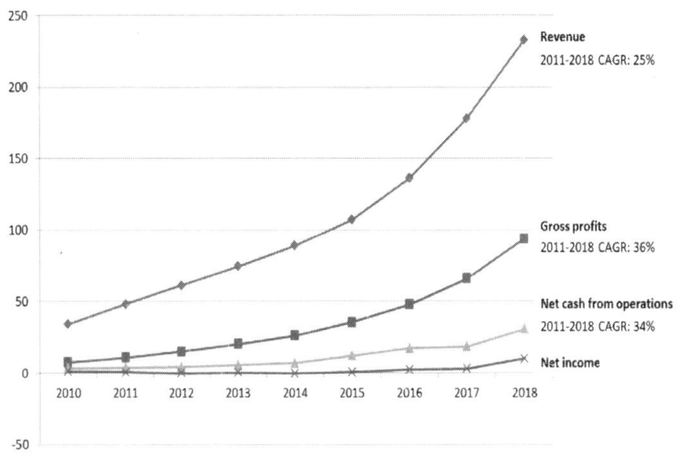

Let's do the math together. In 2018, Amazon made $232.9Bn revenue. At a gross margin of 40.25%, this translates into $93.7Bn gross margin cash generation in one year alone. From the operating cash flow point of view, Amazon generated $30.7Bn in net cash from operations in 2018.

However, instead of leaving this enormous cash as profits on its financial statement, Amazon has been consistently and massively investing gross margin cash into technology ($28.8 billion in R and D expenses), platform and infrastructure ($13.4Bn in capital expenditure) to fund its exponentially fast scaling.[18]

Over a 7-year time period from 2011 to 2017, Amazon invested over $150 billion worldwide in fulfillment networks, transportation capabilities, and technology infrastructure, including AWS data centers.[19]

Why? From our earlier analysis, you will know this is deliberately done in the spirit of scale and speed, i.e., to drive continued growth in the number of customers, customer data, improvement of end-to-end customer experience, and to **sustain large-scale barriers and**

reinforce unmatchable competitive advantages in the platform, the infrastructure (the last mile delivery) and the digital core competence.

Viewed in this light, one can clearly see the consistent underlying logic that cuts through Amazon's 25-year journey—one that is amazing while at the same time seemingly confusing and marked by continuous exploration and expansion. In fact, no matter what Amazon did, does or will do, it has and will always derive from its core principles: customer obsession, relentless drive to invent, long-term thinking, and prioritization of cash generation. Amazon's remarkable consistency to these principles from Day 1 has positioned the company to create an historic variety of businesses at a global scale. Few people recognize the tight underlying linkage among all pieces as part of a holistic self-reinforcing dynamic model that is able to capitalize the new concepts of platform, ecosystem, and infrastructure in the digital age, continuously strengthen the digital core competence, drastically defy traditional laws of diminishing returns, and reliably delivers enormous cash generation and shareholder value creation.

HOW TO MAKE IT WORK?

To conceive a business model is one thing; to make it work, to get it up and running, continuously evolving and upgrading is another. Countless intriguing business plans, impressive blue-prints and brilliant game-changing ideas never hit the road, or fail to deliver. Why was the Amazon leadership team able to pull this off?

Many business leaders and entrepreneurs are super strong and devoted in business, but have neither the will nor the skill in organizational management. Once business outgrows personal and organizational capabilities, growth momentum will slow down, and in some cases, the companies may even collapse.

Bezos is the opposite. As founder and CEO of Amazon, he has the rare combination of a visionary leader and a down-to-earth builder obsessed with the organization and how it should be run. He is the mastermind behind the design of Amazon's digital management system, and also the field marshal who forcefully and personally drives the enforcement.

Why so much effort personally? Because Bezos knows too well that a business model without the right management system won't fly.

****

To realize his dream, Bezos needs to build a continuous invention machine, a consistent and effective mechanism of high-quality and high-velocity decision-making, and an AI-powered data and metrics system to track, measure, analyze real-time data and automate routine decisions for ultimate speed and quality, while at the same time vigilantly guard against bureaucracy and complacency. Otherwise his company will creep onto the treacherous slippery slope called "Day 2," thus burying his aspirations of a forever-Day-1 organization.

This is an endeavor way beyond any single person's capacity. It requires the combined force of a team or an army of the right people to create a "phenomenon of nature."

So who are the right people by the Amazon standards, and how to find them, motivate them and retain them? In the next chapter, let's explore how Amazon builds its **continuous bar-raising** talent pool.

REFLECTIONS AND IDEAS TO CONSIDER FOR YOUR COMPANY

CHAPTER HIGHLIGHTS

BUILDING BLOCK 2

Amazon's talent pool is carefully defined, meticulously documented, and rigorously chosen; coupled with complete end-to-end follow-through and feedback to ensure **continuous bar-raising**, both for the talent pool itself and for the self-reinforcing mechanism of talent acquisition and retention.

DEFINE THE RIGHT TALENT

The builders
The owners
The mental toughness

RECRUIT THE RIGHT TALENT

The bar raisers
The rigorous process
The self-selecting mechanism

MOTIVATE AND RETAIN THE RIGHT TALENT

Dreamland for the builders
Paradise for the ambitious
The high standards

FIGHT FOR THE TOP TALENT

BUILDING BLOCK 2:

CONTINUOUS BAR-RAISING TALENT POOL

History tells us that most people who have come up with fascinating new ideas have failed. Why? Because they remained primarily as dreamers themselves, and lacked the solid grip on execution required to convert their dreams into reality as builders do.

Bezos is rare among visionaries, for in addition to having 20-20 insight into what will transpire, he is also a builder and also a man of his words. His relentless commitment to excellent execution enables him to cut through all factors on the surface and get straight into the single most important factor accountable for success: **the right people**.

That's why back in 1994, before informing his colleagues at D. E. Shaw and Co. of his decision to leave his lucrative job on Wall Street to start his own company, Bezos made a special trip from New York to California to conduct his first round of interviews for experienced programmers. Luckily he lured Shel Kaphan, a startup veteran and a technical genius, to be the first employee of Amazon. Since then he has consistently filled the talent pipeline with individuals who have provided immeasurable value to the company.

It's also why if you ask Bezos what the most important decision is at Amazon, his answer will be and has always been from the very beginning: hiring the right talent.

Many Amazon people will recall Bezos repeatedly telling them so. In fact, Bezos has gone so far as to say that "It's better to let the perfect person go than to hire the wrong person and to deal with the ramifications."[1]

Why? Because Bezos believes that your people are your company.

The wrong person not only cannot deliver his due duties by the required standards, but also has negative impacts on others around him or her. While keeping a wrong person clearly hurts performance and team morale, correcting a hiring mistake could be even more costly, time-consuming, and emotionally wrenching. Such a dilemma, by itself, is an excruciating drill familiar to many leaders.

Bezos is not alone on this.

We (Ram and Julia) strongly agree with this belief. As Ram frequently puts it, **nothing overcomes the wrong person**. If you have the wrong person on a job, no matter how much coaching, training or developing you pour into him or her, the return on the enormous time, money, and efforts will most likely be minimal—if not negative.

Tony Hsieh, Zappos CEO, also shares this view. He has even quantified the cost of hiring mistakes at a staggering price tag of $100M; and is probably the reason why he invented a surprisingly unorthodox but effective policy, in which Zappos will pay new hires $2,000 to quit.

Bezos, an eager learner, saw huge value in this ingenious approach and implemented a "Pay to Quit" program at Amazon fulfillment centers. In his 2013 Shareholder Letter, he explained how it works.

> *"It was invented by the clever people at Zappos, and the Amazon fulfillment centers have been iterating on it. Pay to Quit is pretty simple. Once a year, we offer to pay our associates to quit. The first year the offer is made, it's for $2,000. Then it goes up one thousand dollars a year until it reaches $5,000. The headline on the offer is 'Please Don't Take This Offer.' We hope they don't take the offer;*

we want them to stay. Why do we make this offer? The goal is to encourage folks to take a moment and think about what they really want. In the long run, an employee staying somewhere they don't want to be isn't healthy for the employee or the company."

Bezos deeply understands the importance of talent. Dating back to 1997, the last (but not the least) point within the famous 9-point management and decision-making approach stated in his first Shareholder Letter is on talent:

"We will continue to focus on hiring and retaining versatile and talented employees, and continue to weight their compensation to stock options rather than cash. We know our success will be largely affected by our ability to attract and retain a motivated employee base, each of whom must think like, and therefore must actually be, an owner."

So what has Amazon done to make sure that they only attract and retain the right talent? In the first place, what is "right" by Amazon's standards?

DEFINE THE RIGHT TALENT

Depending on the context, the company, and the specific situation, the definition of the "right talent" can vary widely. Despite all these essential differences, in order to truly compete on talent in a fundamental way, defining the right talent must be done in a manner that is clear, specific and consistent, so that the entire organization is able to follow the same criteria and fight against inevitable deviation along the way.

On this front, Bezos has been clear and consistent from the very beginning. He looks for builders who can make things happen, who can think and behave like owners—the type of people who display a sense of "true ownership."

THE BUILDERS

On multiple occasions over the years, Bezos has described the profile of the "builders." The most recent version is in his 2018 Shareholder Letter:

> *"Builders are people who are* ***curious, explorers. They like to invent.*** *Even when they're experts, they are 'fresh' with a beginner's mind. They see the way we do things as just the way we do things now. A builder's mentality helps us approach big, hard-to-solve opportunities with a humble conviction that* ***success can come through iteration****: invent, launch, reinvent, relaunch, start over, rinse, repeat, again and again. They know the path to success is anything but straight."(Our emphasis).*

In an interview with Charlie Rose in 2012, Bezos said that he considers himself as a builder, and stated with overt pride and joy that there are "a lot of builders at Amazon."

As a man who chooses his words carefully, Bezos is sharing a powerful message here. Read his definition carefully, at least twice, and then take a minute to imagine what a lot of builders would do and could achieve together.

In these builders lie the powerful engine, the resilient spirit and the unwavering determination of Amazon's customer-obsessed business model, continuous ground-breaking invention machine, high-quality, and high-velocity decision-making and forever-Day-1 vitality.

THE OWNERS

Among the 14 Leadership Principles at Amazon, right after the number one principle, Customer Obsession, comes Ownership. Leaders are owners. They **think long-term** and don't sacrifice long-term value for short-term results. They act on behalf of the entire company, beyond just their own team. **They never say, "that's not my job."**[2]

How important is true ownership for Amazon and for Bezos? This value is embodied in two quotes from his Shareholder Letters: "it's all about the long term" in 1997, and "long-term thinking is both a requirement and an outcome of true ownership" in 2003.[3]

Regrettably, some executives in traditional companies behave like tenants: they fail to act on behalf of the entire company, not even of their own team, and pursue their own personal interests instead. For them, it is not only unreasonable, but also utterly insane to do the following:

- **Hire and develop the best.** They probably ask themselves: what if those people outshine themselves and become more of a threat than an asset to them?
- **Frugality:** why bother to control expenses? It is not their money. Also even if they do not squander the money, someone else is bound to.
- **Dive deep:** why use so much personal time and energy to stay connected to the details? If something goes wrong, it's someone else's problem.
- **Have backbone; disagree and commit:** why seek the trouble to challenge others or even the boss? It is uncomfortable and exhausting, and more importantly, detrimental to personal relationships and career advancement.
- **Deliver results:** why should they always rise to the occasion and never settle despite all setbacks? Isn't that the boss' job? Why do bosses get higher pay and better benefits? That's exactly the time they should put their necks in the noose.

By the logic of tenants, these behaviors are indeed insane. These observable behaviors are the test of true ownership. That's what Amazon stated in the Leadership Principles, number six (hire and develop the best), ten (frugality), twelve (dive deep), thirteen (have backbone; disagree and commit), and fourteen (deliver results) respectively.

Without a true sense of ownership, none of these behaviors mentioned above would happen. Now you probably understand why Bezos would repeatedly elaborate the concept of "owners" at all kinds of venues, especially in all-hands meetings at Amazon.

THE MENTAL TOUGHNESS

While certain required qualities may not be explicitly called for as job prerequisites, it is clear that to become a builder with true ownership by Bezos' standards, and to survive and thrive at Amazon, you must have an enormous amount of mental toughness.

Without mental toughness, why would someone choose a hard-to-solve problem (or in Bezos' term "opportunity") when there is an easy way out? How could they face failure, numerous times, and still choose to "reinvent, relaunch, start over, rinse, and repeat, again and again"?

Without mental toughness, how could they survive the uncomfortable and sometimes exhausting process of being questioned, challenged and even ranted at? How could they, despite all the setbacks, still rise to the occasion and never settle?

As former Amazon executive John Rossman put it:[4]

> *"If you want to succeed in Jeff's relentless and fiercely competitive world, you cannot:*
>
> - Feel sorry for yourself
> - Give away your power
> - Shy away from change
> - Waste energy on things you cannot control
> - Worry about pleasing others
> - Fear taking calculated risks
> - Dwell on the past
> - Make the same mistakes over and over
> - Resent others' success
> - Give up after failure
> - Feel the world owes you anything; or
> - Expect immediate results
>
> *The most successful are those who can excel in the pressure cooker, week in and week out, shaking off the occasional failure and the subsequent tongue-lashing, put their heads down, and keep on driving."*

Bezos has persistently demonstrated tremendous mental toughness himself. But not everyone worth employing can reach that standard. The examples are countless, including his decision to pursue Prime "almost alone,"[5] his decision to pursue the crazy hardware idea which later became Kindle despite overwhelming resistance, and stretching all the way back to the beginning when he took 60 meetings to raise the first $1 million.

RECRUIT THE RIGHT TALENT

While defining the right talent is a key first step, how does Amazon follow through by recruiting the people systematically?

Chip Bayer's 1999 *Wired* magazine article revealed an early look into Bezos' unique and rigorous approach of recruiting.

> *"He (Bezos) also turned hiring staff into a Socratic test. 'Jeff was very, very picky,' says Nicholas Lovejoy, who joined Amazon.com as its fifth employee in June 1995. In endless hiring meetings, Bezos, after interviewing the candidate himself, would grill every other interviewer, occasionally constructing elaborate charts on a whiteboard detailing the job seeker's qualifications. If he ferreted out the slightest doubt, rejection usually followed. 'One of his mottos was that every time we hired someone, he or she should raise the bar for the next hire, so that the overall talent pool was always improving,' Lovejoy says."*

Bezos strongly believes in the importance of recruiting the right talent for business success. "**Setting the bar high in our approach to hiring** has been, and will continue to be, **the single most important element of Amazon.com's success.**"[6] (Our emphasis).

When Amazon was in its early days, it was still possible for Bezos to do recruiting personally. No longer. Amazon is now a burgeoning 750,000-people organization, so how to reinforce such rigor and maintain such a high bar — not only across the globe but also down to each new hire?

THE BAR RAISERS

Bar raisers are indeed a unique feature of Amazon's recruiting practices. Without exception, there will be a bar raiser among all interviewers whom a candidate will meet during the recruiting process.

Bar raisers are carefully selected individuals who are meticulously trained to be the stewards of Amazon's leadership principles. Their mission is to ensure that the bar is never lowered due to pressing business urgency, to make the final and right hiring decisions and to strive for continuous rising of the bar. In many ways, they act on behalf of the Amazon leadership team as the final line of defense in recruiting.

No doubt it is a big honor to be a named bar raiser at Amazon. To qualify, individuals must be builders with true ownership themselves, and must have demonstrated a strong historical track record in terms of successful recruiting and retention.

Bar raisers are usually assigned to recruiting outside their own businesses, so that they could stay independent from urgent business need.

They have three tasks at hand. The first is to evaluate, using Amazon's Leadership Principles as the yardstick, whether candidates have long-term potential at Amazon and whether they can raise the bar.

The second is to conduct the post-interview drilling with each interviewer, as Bezos did before, so that all observations, assessments, considerations, and doubts can be fully explored and thoroughly examined to arrive at a correct decision.

The third is to help hiring managers and other interviewers prepare for interviews, to ensure consistency in the high bar and, most importantly, to provide written feedback.

THE RIGOROUS PROCESS

Giving that recruiting the right talent is regarded as the most important decision at Amazon, the company has made huge investment in terms of team's time and energy into getting this right.

At Amazon, in addition to conducting the interview, each interviewer is required to document all key interview findings, detailed assessments, and judgment calls (a vote on whether to hire or not) into the system. Interviewers for the next round are required to review all the previous findings before their own interviews, so that they can adjust their line of questioning accordingly.

After the interview, the work is far from done. The post-interview drilling with the bar raiser or sometimes Bezos himself can be as intensive and time-consuming as—if not more than—the interview itself. What questions were asked, and why? What answers were given? How did the assessment and judgment get formed? No stone will be left unturned. All details will be explored, examined and extensively documented.

Once all the interviews are done, the hiring manager and the bar raiser review all the notes and the votes. If there is a need for a collective briefing, all the interviewers are required to attend. Despite strong advocacy from the business side on the grounds of urgency and/or necessity, the bar raiser retains veto power to reject a candidate. As mentioned above, the bar raiser has the obligation to provide written feedback to all.

After the final decision is made, and the new hire gets on board, the interviewers and the bar raiser are still not off the hook. The follow-through of new hires begins immediately: how well each new hire performs, how long each stays at Amazon, and how accurate the judgment of each interviewer is are all tracked, well documented and made known to the relevant parties.

This impressive set of practices supporting the rigorous recruiting process demonstrates that Amazon has indeed invested enormous efforts in recruiting. So what's the return on this particular investment? Is it worthwhile?

For Bezos, the answer is yes, unequivocally. In fact this is a deliberately designed self-reinforcing mechanism to ensure rigorous enforcement of consistent standards and continuous bar-rising in both talent pool and institutional recruiting capabilities.

A contrast with how recruiting is normally done in most traditional companies can help you, in a big way, put Amazon's unique, effective, and methodical approach into perspective and appreciate the mastermind behind it

In most companies, recruiting requests are generated by various departments or businesses, and so a lack of consistency in setting the bar company-wide creeps in from the starting point. Since everyone conducts their own interviews, some urgent hiring requests are processed in haste. Personal preferences and immediate needs tend to dictate how the hiring process takes place, leading to little or no consideration of the candidate's actual fit or long-term prospects within the company. Thus the bar, even if high in the beginning, could be compromised or bent by short-term necessity.

As a result, unlike the continuous bar-raising at Amazon, which happens intentionally and by design, the hiring standards at most companies (assuming they even have them) will eventually erode.

Moreover, at most companies, job interviews are rarely documented, and when they are, done so poor or so generic that they are almost useless. People find it difficult to trace back how the interviews were conducted, how the candidates were assessed, and how the final decisions were made.

Once the new hires come on board, the responsibility shifts from recruiting to training, and then to performance management. No matter how poor the performances of new hires are, no one would be able to figure out who was actually involved in the hiring process, explore what factors had been missed, or examine how to improve next time, even if they bothered to do so.

Since there is no feedback to recruiters and interviewers, they cannot improve their skills or practices.

THE SELF-SELECTING MECHANISM

Amazon aspires to make its hiring as frustration-free to job seekers as its shopping experience to its customers. That's why Amazon has posted helpful guides on the company websites, sharing tips including the following:

TIP 1: Leadership Principles. "The best way a candidate can prepare for an interview is to consider how they've applied the Leadership Principles during their previous professional experience."

TIP 2: Failures. "We encourage all candidates to have specific examples of times when they have taken risks, failed or made mistakes, and grown or succeeded as a result." Why so much emphasis on failure? Because failure is an integral part of innovation and invention.

TIP 3: Writing. "For some roles, we may ask a candidate to complete a writing sample." Why? Because PowerPoint has long been banned at Amazon and they use narrative-style memos instead.

While tips such as these are considerate and helpful to the candidates, they are also carefully designed to benefit Amazon: the subtle beauty is that they are designed to weed out the non-fit from the very beginning. Those people who have studied Amazon's Leadership Principles and thought through past failures and prepared writing samples will inevitably end up assessing their own personalities, preferences, and competencies during the process and seriously evaluate whether they are the right fit for Amazon. In short, Amazon's transparency about its talent criteria has transformed recruiting into a "self-selecting" exercise.

Beyond creating a process to maximize "fit," Amazon also designed its compensation scheme along the same line of thought. The objective is to seek out the real builders with true ownership and long-term thinking.

Amazon is notoriously famous for its frugality. The generous perks offered by other digital giants, such as Google and Facebook, are apparently out of the question at Amazon. Amazon employees are even required to pay partially for their own parking at work.

In lieu of high salaries, compensation has been titled towards stock options rather than cash—which Bezos pointed out in his initial 1997 Shareholder Letter. The salaries of Jeff Wilke, CEO of Worldwide Consumer, and Andy Jassy, CEO of AWS were only $175,000. In addition, Amazon deliberately avoids giving bonus as Bezos believes that it is not good for internal collaboration. Executive bonuses were terminated in 2010.[7]

At Amazon, the majority of compensation is instead stock based. The vesting period is also heavily tilted towards the long term: 5% for the first year, 15% for the second year, and 20% each for the next four half-year periods. This is very different from the usual vesting schedule of 25% for each year during the four-year period for most high-tech companies.

For anyone who takes his or her career seriously and thus spends some time on learning about Amazon, including what kind of people the company is looking for, and what kind of compensation package the company is offering, the conclusion is clear: Amazon is probably the last place to go for those who seek short-term cash, generous or even luxurious benefits, and comfortable low-challenge day-to-day work.

Bingo! This is exactly the conclusion that Amazon would like those job applicants to draw by themselves, because they are the wrong people by Amazon's standards. This is what Bezos means by "self-selecting."

MOTIVATE AND RETAIN THE RIGHT TALENT

Given that Amazon's bar is so high and continuously rising, and the short-term cash compensation is not so lucrative, how can Amazon motivate and retain the real builders with true ownership and mental toughness on a long-term basis?

The answer lies in two aspects: what they love, and what they hate.

DREAMLAND FOR THE BUILDERS

What do builders hate most? Bureaucracy. It is slow; it is suffocating; and in many cases it prevents them from making things happen in the way they like.

For Bezos, the abhorrence of bureaucracy is personal. It goes all the way back to his childhood. Bezos' grandpa, Lawrence Preston "Pop" Gise, a real builder, strongly held the same view. During World War II, Gise was a lieutenant commander in the U.S. Navy, and then worked at DARPA in the late 1950s. At the height of his career, he managed a staff of 26,000 people at the Atomic Energy Commission. "In 1968, at the age of fifty-three, Pop Gise resigned from the U.S. Atomic Energy Commission over a bureaucratic squabble with his bosses in Washington."[8] It is not hard to imagine, even today, the seething anger that let him to quit on the spot.

Gise was a towering figure in Bezos' life. He was probably the first and foremost mentor to Bezos. "He instilled in Bezos the values of self-reliance and resourcefulness, as well as a visceral distaste for inefficiency."[9]

A bureaucratic organization is filled with complacency. Everything seems to move in slow motion, from decision-making to execution of ideas. Everything becomes blurry, especially regarding results, performance, accountability, and action items. Everything needs to follow a Standard Operating Procedure (SOP) with little or no room to deviate or innovate, or go through a complicated process and lengthy approval chain.

Such an atmosphere is anathema to builders, who love to invent, and to try unconventional ways. They have little patience and want to jump in and make things happen.

Above all, builders love challenges. The problems that appear to be hard-to-solve or even impossible for many people represent something entirely different to the real builders. They see these problems as exciting opportunities, the best thrillers and the most fun part of the job.

When approached by Amazon back in 1999, Jeff Wilke was a vice president at Allied Signal, reporting directly to the legendary CEO, Larry Bossidy (who co-authored with Ram, the global bestseller *Execution*). What got Wilke excited about joining Amazon was "the chance of building a unique distribution network and define a nascent industry, an opportunity that simply didn't exist at Allied Signal."[10]. What's unique? Something that was then non-existent. This daunting challenge may scare away many, but it is precisely what attracts the real builders.

When Steve Kessel was abruptly called by Bezos one day in 2004 and asked to take over the company's fledgling digital efforts and build brand new things, which later became Kindle, he immediately "got excited by the challenge."[11] Unlike today, Amazon had zero experience in devices at the time.

Andy Jassy shared his thoughts on this in 2013:

> *"I can't think of another place . . . . that thinks long-term rather than optically for a quarter, or that looks at an area of business (or customer experience) and doesn't let itself get blocked by existing convention, or that gives people who deliver a chance to try any new entrepreneurial venture that makes sense regardless of their experience level in that area, or that hires builders who are unleashed to go change the world, or has such a sharp, inventive, big-thinking, high bias for action, collegial, hungry, and delivery oriented culture. It's why I'm still here 16 years later . . . .* ***Amazon is a builder's dream****, and if you want a chance to change the world in a pervasive way, there is no better place." (Our emphasis)*

Andy Jassy is still with Amazon today, 22 years later. Jeff Wilke and Steve Kessel are still with Amazon today after 20 years. In fact, among the entire 18-member S-team (Amazon's core executive team, including Bezos, and his direct reports and selective two-level-down executives), half have been with the company for 20 years or longer, including Jeff Wilke (1999), Andy Jassy (1997), Jeff Blackburn (1998), David Zapolsky (1999), Russ Grandinetti (1998), Steve Kessel (1999), Charlie Bell (1998), Paul Kotas (1999), and Peter DeSantis (1998).

For a company with only a 25-year history, this is beyond amazing.

PARADISE FOR THE AMBITIOUS

For those young and ambitious souls who are committed to accelerating personal growth and eager for an entrepreneurial experience, Amazon is their paradise.

At Amazon, new hires are pleasantly surprised at how much ownership they can have from the start. When they are assigned to a project team, they will be exposed to and engaged in all functions involved, and make decisions and build products that could potentially impact millions of customers.

In his 2014 Shareholder Letter, Bezos wrote about Prime Now, the new one-hour delivery service, with noticeable pride:

> *"Prime Now .... was launched only* ***111 days*** *after it was dreamed up. In that time, a small team built a customer-facing app, secured a location for an urban warehouse, determined which 25,000 items to sell, got those items stocked, recruited and on-boarded new staff, tested, iterated, designed new software for internal use – both a warehouse management system and a driver-facing app – and launched in time for the holidays."*

If you were lucky enough to be on that team from the beginning, your personal learning curve and increasing versatility would have gone far beyond your wildest imagination. Such an experience is what attracts and retains the young and ambitious.

Of course, such accelerated learning and unparalleled versatility may not suit everyone. Some former employees at Amazon have complained that they "let engineers do so many things."

Again, this is how the game is designed. "Self-selecting", remember?

THE HIGH STANDARDS

Other than such an accelerated learning experience, high standards have also played an important role. "Insist on the Highest Standards" is the number seven Leadership Principle at Amazon. It reads:

> *"Leaders have relentlessly high standards—many people may think these standards are unreasonably high. Leaders are continually raising the bar and driving their teams to deliver high-quality products, services, and processes. Leaders ensure that defects do not get sent down the line and that problems are fixed so they stay fixed."*

Why the high, or even highest, standards? Because Bezos believes that "people are drawn to high standards – they help with recruiting and retention."[12]

Indeed, for the young and ambitious, what could be a better way to help them grow than setting the unreasonably high or the highest standards?

FIGHT FOR THE TOP TALENTS

Bezos understands that a superb job in defining, recruiting, motivating and retaining the right talent is indeed very precious, but not sufficient. Beyond this, Amazon needs to continuously and proactively seek and fight for the top talent.

The unique challenge of attracting top talents lies in an interesting paradox: on the one hand, they are usually not the active job seekers, thus technically off the market; on the other hand, they are always closely coveted and quietly but heatedly chased by many.

Fighting for the top talent is a CEO job that cannot and should not be completely delegated to HR. For those top talents, direct interactions with the CEO, the founder, chairman, and the top executives could play a decisive role in their final decisions.

Take the courting of Rick Dalzell, a former Walmart executive, for example. During his 10-year tenure at Amazon, Dalzell was Bezos' long-term right-hand man. Besides his CIO job, he also played a pivotal role in developing people and organizations. He brought in the right talent at the right time and developed many more people along the way. Andy Jassy, the current CEO of AWS, is among the many Dalzell coached.

It actually took Bezos more than half a year to win over Dalzell. Bezos and Joy Covey, Amazon's then-CFO, started their courtship of Dalzell in early 1997. At that time, he was a senior executive at Walmart. Several initial attempts were futile as Dalzell turned them down, repeatedly.

When their first meeting finally took place, it seemed to be particularly cursed, marked by Dalzell's double misfortune of luggage lost by the airline and coffee spilled on him by Bezos.

Yet Bezos is not a man who would give up easily. He continued to push ahead with his own brand of intensity and relentlessness.

He asked Covey to call Dalzell's wife every few weeks. He lined up the acclaimed venture capitalist John Doerr to meet with Dalzell. He even flew to Bentonville, where Walmart headquarters and Dalzell's family were located, with Covey on a surprise trip to invite Dalzell out for dinner.

All these efforts eventually paid off. Dalzell agreed to join Amazon after that dinner. But the joy of victory was short-lived, as Dalzell later changed his mind due to the seemingly impossible drudgery of moving his entire family from Bentonville to Seattle.

Despite this major setback, Bezos actually succeeded in planting the seed of Amazon in Dalzell's heart. As time went by, the seed started to grow and flourish.

Eventually Dalzell's wife, who was in fact part of the Amazon recruiting team by then, convinced him to pull the trigger. Dalzell joined Amazon as CIO in August 1997.

This anecdote illustrates that fighting for these top talents is never an easy task. In addition to you, the top players will constantly get calls from other potential employers, while at the same time their existing employer will also charm them, incentivize them or even coerce them to stay. You need to be as tenacious, relentless and resourceful as Bezos was in the case of fighting for Dalzell.

All your efforts on people will be well spent. Just as Bezos said, at the end of the day, your people are you company.

* * * * * * * *

Among the six building blocks of the Amazon Management System, there are two **foundational** ones. Without these two, all others will crumble and the entire system will collapse.

So what are the two? The Continuous Bar-Raising Talent Pool (Building Block 2) elaborated in this chapter is one, and the other is the AI-Powered Data and Metrics System (Building Block 3).

It is of pivotal importance to running the day-to-day at Amazon for operational excellence, and to freeing up more organizational energy for continuous improvement, innovation and invention.

What is an AI-powered data and metrics system, and how does it work? Let's explore in the next chapter.

REFLECTIONS AND IDEAS TO CONSIDER FOR YOUR COMPANY

CHAPTER HIGHLIGHTS

BUILDING BLOCK 3

Amazon's data and metrics system is ultra-detailed, cross-silo, cross-layer, end-to-end, real-time, input-oriented and AI-powered, therefore everything can be tracked, measured, and analyzed in real time with anomaly detected, insights generated and routine decisions automated.

THE ANSWER STARTS WITH NUMBERS

Ultra-detailed
End-to-end
Real-time
Track inputs
Trust but verify

THE LIBERATING DATA AND METRICS

The executives
The frontline people
The continuous bar-raising

THE POWERFUL AI-POWERED TOOLS

The examples
The automation enables

BUILDING BLOCK 3:

AI-POWERED DATA AND METRICS SYSTEM

Running Amazon, the gigantic business empire with unprecedented complexity from drastically different businesses, from vastly spanned geographies worldwide and from the massive size and scope of operations, is no doubt a daunting challenge for many.

If you were charged with such important obligation, you would probably be deeply buried to the neck in administering the day-to-day.

To the huge surprise of all, Jeff Bezos, founder and CEO of Amazon, actually rarely spends time on day-to-day considerations. "I try to organize my personal time so that I live mostly about 2 to 3 years out."[1] He also requests that his top leaders do the same. Ram saw similar mindset in former chairman and CEO of GE, Jack Welch.

Is this because Bezos is super hands-off? Absolutely not. On the normal spectrum of hands on vs. hands off, Bezos would perhaps be the one to redefine diving deep into details by magnitude.

If this is true, how to reconcile this perplexing paradox?

Without digitization, one could not do that. Bezos' secret lies in the Amazon world-class standard-setting AI-powered data and metrics system, in which everything that matters can be tracked, measured and analyzed, with insights generated and routine decisions automated.

Such a system not only liberates Bezos, executives, and frontline employees at Amazon from managing routine daily chores and the inevitable bureaucracy associated, but also enables powerful AI-powered tools-that are fundamental to the Amazon management system.

THE ANSWER STARTS WITH NUMBERS

Jeff Bezos is a man of numbers. This is his unique way of understanding the world, having fun in life and running business at Amazon.

When he was a little boy, Bezos would go on long-distance driving adventures with his grandparents. During those long hours on the road, he would kill time by doing minor arithmetic problems and making estimates. One specific case Bezos mentioned during his speech on 2010 Princeton Commencement was that after hearing an advertisement campaign about smoking which stated that each puff of a cigarette would cut short people's life span by a few minutes, he proudly told his grandma, "At two minutes per puff, you've taken nine years off your life!"

Sounds incredible? It may seem incredible to most of us, but this was simple and straight-forward for Bezos. Building on the estimates of daily consumption of cigarettes, and the number of puffs per cigarette, he quickly did the math in his head. (On that day, Bezos learned a valuable life lesson from his grandpa that it's harder to be kind than clever.)

In terms of founding and managing Amazon, a fast-expanding giant woven into almost all aspects of the economy and people's lives, Bezos followed the same line of thinking. At Amazon, when Bezos throws a question at you, there is no wriggle room for obfuscation or buzzwords. If you dare to try, he will rant at you, ruthlessly, "the answer starts with a number!" Everyone at Amazon knows the famous line by W. Edwards Deming, "In God we trust, all others must bring data."[2]

For many people working at Amazon, the first thing they do every day is look at the numbers. Armed with smartphones, many of them start this daily ritual even before getting out of bed. They have become masters of cutting through a bevy of numbers to know what is really happening.

Just as Bezos has his unique standards to define the right talent for Amazon, as described in the previous chapter, he also has his unique standards to define what the robust data and metrics are.

ULTRA-DETAILED

Execution is about knowing and delivering details. Amazon's level of details for data and metrics is magnitudes beyond many people's wildest imagination. "Shock" is usually the first reaction of many outside Amazon.

If you were asked to pick a location for a new data center, how many factors would you consider? About five, ten, twenty, or dozens? Amazon used a checklist of 282 metrics when choosing its first data center in China, according to Mr. Wan Xinheng, mayor of Zhongwei, a small city located in the west of China, where Amazon built its first data center in the country back in 2015. In an interview in 2016, Mr. Wan said that he was clearly shocked.

If you were to set annual goals for your company, how many items would you list? About five, ten, twenty, or dozens? Amazon nailed down 452 detailed goals for 2010, as stated in Bezos' 2009 Shareholder Letter. But goals, by themselves, are not enough. Amazon also specified owners, deliverables, and targeted completion dates for each.

If you were in charge of the third-party book category at Amazon, how many metrics would you look at each day? About 5, 10, 20, or dozens? Amazon compiled 25 pages of various metrics, such as:[3]

- Order defect rate (ODR): the percentage of orders with negative feedback from customers, be it an explicit complaint, a low rating, or a dispute.
- Pre-fulfillment cancellation rate: the percentage of orders cancelled before shipment.
- Late shipment rate: the percentage of orders that arrived later than the committed date.

- Refund rate: the percentage of orders that resulted in refunds for any possible reason.
- Contacts per order: the average number of all human interactions for each order.
- The best-selling books, key words, writers, publishing houses, and third parties.
- The most-searched books, key words, writers, publishing houses, and third parties.
- The time required to load a webpage.

Just imagine such detailed metrics, two to three magnitudes beyond the normal definition of detailed, going on for 25 pages.

Would you find 25 pages too much? As a matter of fact, this is already a scaled-back version from the original 70-plus-page list. Of course, if you want to deep dive into some metrics, you can always log on to Amazon's internal system to fully indulge yourself in an ocean of data and metrics.

END-TO-END

In most traditional companies, data collection is broken down by silo, by layer, and by actual involvement. Each division or function can see data generated and collected only within its own domain of business operations. For example, sales may see sales numbers, marketing may see marketing expenses, production may see production orders and finance may see inventory turns, bottom lines and cash generation. However, it would be extremely hard to link all these data points and figure out, at each SKU level, which ones were the best in generating cash flow and net profits.

In these types of organizations, it is almost impossible to get data from other silos. Information sharing may be thwarted by a number of reasons such as concerns about confidentiality, lack of authorization or reluctance stemming from personal grudges, as well as other obstacles disguised by delay, distortion, or purposeful omission of critical pieces of information. The list of legitimate reasons will be long, and the list of deliberate and delicate excuses will be even longer. Why? Because in many cases, information has become the basis of power.

That's why when traditional companies embark on the journey of digitization, data transparency is usually one of the first steps. As one chairman repeatedly reminded everyone during an extended executive workshop on digitization, there should be "no more hoarding of data."

As we mentioned in the chapter on "Building Block 1: Customer-Obsessed Business Model," data is the new equity in the digital age. In this sense, all data belongs to the entire company, not any individual or any division.

At Amazon, a small team is bestowed with the end-to-end responsibility for one product or one service. How to ensure that this team does a good job? After ensuring the selection of the best people, the next most important crucial enabler is the availability of end-to-end data that is not segregated by silo nor by function. Without such data support, running a business would be as difficult as maneuvering in a pitch-dark mansion.

In this sense, the transparency of end-to-end data is an effective forcing mechanism in dismantling silos and enabling end-to-end accountability.

REAL-TIME

In many companies, business reviews are held quarterly or monthly, with a delay of ten days or more due to the time needed for accounting proceedings. As a result, it is common for the Q1 reviews to be held around April 10 and the May review around June 10.

In one real-case example from our experience, the quarterly review of a company's key account business was held on April 15. During the meeting, the VP of key account business reviewed with his team the Q1 performance vs. budget for each of the top 20 accounts. For those with big gaps, he probed the data from the quarterly down to monthly performances and found out that, for one particular account, January sales met the budget, but sales suddenly dropped in February and March. He questioned the person in charge about the potential causes, brainstormed with the team about how to fix them, and made decisions on four action items right on the spot.

What do you think about this VP? Ready to sing his praise for having a nose for details, a bias for action, and the guts to make decisions on the spot? He is a great leader, right? He may be a great leader by the traditional standards, but such a way of running a business is woefully inadequate for winning in the digital age. Any actions starting on April 15 are already too late by two-and-a-half months.

At Amazon, such data is tracked on a real-time basis with no time lag. Relevant people can review the results daily, hourly, or by the second. Armed with real-time data and metrics system, the person in charge of that particular account mentioned above could have probably detected the anomaly by herself as early as within the first few days of February, or even the last few days of January, and could have adjusted by oneself or with one-level approval at most. No need to waste two-and-a-half months. In some cases, your company's fate can be sealed within two-and-a-half months or even just two-and-a-half days.

TRACK INPUTS

This is probably the most unique aspect of Amazon's data and metrics system.

When setting goals, most companies focus on revenue growth, margins, and net profits. However, among Amazon's 452 goals for 2010, "The word revenue is used eight times and free cash flow is used only four times . . . .the terms net income, gross profit or margin, and operating profit are not used once.[4]"

Why? Revenue, growth, margins, and net profits are outputs. Amazon believes that to ensure good outputs, one needs to get to the bottom of the issue and seriously track the inputs.

Why does Amazon track the time required to load a webpage? Because its data analytics shows that "even a minuscule 0.1-second delay in a webpage loading can translate into a 1 percent drop in customer activity."[5]

Why does Amazon track the metric of contacts per order? Because each contact, i.e., human interaction with the customers, can reveal a potential system defect and clearly has costs, big or small. In fact, by tracking and then aggressively reducing contacts per order by 90%, Amazon significantly improved its profitability in 2002, i.e., turning positive in operating profits for the first time in the company's history.[6]

TRUST BUT VERIFY

At Amazon, each claim needs to be supported by data and metrics. Unfounded promises will not fly. For those who get caught, their days at Amazon are numbered.

Bezos clearly embodies Amazon's Leadership Principle of Dive Deep, which declares that: Leaders operate at all levels, stay connected to the details, audit frequently, and are skeptical when metrics and anecdotes differ. No task is beneath them, and they would invest time and energy to verify personally.

For example, at an executive meeting during the Christmas season in 2000, Bezos asked the head of the Customer Service Department about customers' wait time. This is a metric of how long customers have to wait before their calls get picked up by a customer service representative. Without offering any supporting evidence, the person replied that it was well under one minute.

How could such a colossal mistake escape Bezos' eagle eye? Using the speakerphone in the middle of the conference room, Bezos dialed the 800 number of Amazon's call center. He even took off his watch to track the time.

Guess how long Bezos waited for his call to get through? Not one minute, not even two minutes, but four-and-a-half minutes. That is 270 seconds. You may take a moment to count from 1 to 270, to get a sense of how long this feels. No doubt, for that particular executive, the collective wait with Bezos and the entire executive team must have felt like an eternity.

Why would Bezos invest the precious four-and-a-half precious minutes of the entire executive team on this seemingly "trivial" detail? Two reasons.

First, to Bezos, who is truly obsessed with customers, this was just the opposite of trivial. In fact, it was paramount to the customers' experience. No customers would call Amazon's call center just for a friendly chat. Usually it was an unpleasant encounter or a frustrating problem that triggered their call. The long wait would simply exacerbate their growing dissatisfaction and mounting anger.

Second, Bezos used this specific example to vividly demonstrate the Dive Deep principle right on the spot, i.e., no task is beneath them, and they should invest time and energy to verify personally. After these painfully long four-and-a-half minutes, everyone on site and everyone who heard about the anecdote would definitely learn the lesson by heart. This is effective coaching in the moment.

How would Bezos himself make a point and support it with bullet-proof evidence?

To illustrate Amazon's pricing objective of "not discounting a small number of products for a limited period of time," but offering "low prices every day and apply them broadly across our entire product range," in his 2002 Shareholder Letter Bezos quoted the results of a price comparison of 100 best-selling books.

To eliminate bias, when picking the 100 best-selling books, he used the list of Amazon's major competitor, you know whom. To ensure representativeness, he examined the composition of these 100 books by category and by format, and had people visit four of their superstores in both Seattle and New York City for price points. Based on the collected information, he compared prices by collective cost, by each title, and by number of books being sold at a discount.

The price-comparison exercise generated the following discoveries:

- "At their stores, these 100 bestselling books cost $1,561. At Amazon.com, the same books cost $1,195 for a total savings of $366, or 23%.

- For 72 of the 100 books, our price was cheaper. On 25 of the books, our price was the same. On 3 of the 100, their prices were better (we subsequently reduced our prices on these three books).
- In these physical-world superstores, only 15 of their 100 titles were discounted — they were selling the other 85 at full list price. At Amazon.com, 76 of the 100 were discounted and 24 were sold at list price."[7]

At Amazon, the ultimate test for the robustness of a data and metrics system is to simply step into the fire. If you can survive the barrage of questions from Bezos and his executives, usually two to three degrees beyond the normal standards of a deep dive, and provide convincing answers supported by solid numbers, it means you have passed.

THE LIBERATING DATA AND METRICS

To define and continuously refine such ultra-detailed, end-to-end (cross-silo and cross-layer), real-time, and input-heavy mazes of metrics, and to continuously track, measure and analyze the massive volume of data by all these metrics, is no piece of cake. It takes heavy investment of money and, more importantly, people's time and energy over many years and at all levels of the organization.

Why has Amazon been so committed to this course? Bezos' strong personal fascination with numbers clearly plays a role here. However, what matters more is the hefty return of such upfront heavy investments.

Armed with the AI-powered data and metrics system, Amazon can liberate all builders at all levels of the organization and at the same time ensure the continuous bar-raising of a forever-Day-1 organization.

THE EXECUTIVES

In most traditional companies, once the business grows bigger, the number of employees expands rapidly as well.

As prescribed by the traditional management theory span of control, the number of subordinates that a manager can effectively supervise is limited. The optimal number varies by the nature of the work at hand, but the range usually goes from 2-3 to 6-8, and rarely expands beyond 10-15. Therefore, understandably, many big companies tend to have six to seven layers of managers. We know a few giants with 10 or more layers.

Equipped with its AI-powered data and metrics system that can continuously track, measure, and analyze business operations, detect anomalies and automate routine decisions using ultra-detailed, end-to-end, real-time and input-heavy metrics, Amazon has actually defied the span of control theory, the cardinal rule of business organization design. Such a data and metrics system significantly minimize the need for physical supervision.

In fact, Amazon defies the rule in such a fundamental way that Jeff Wilke, CEO of Worldwide Consumer, could personally manage 500 project teams. How is that possible? The credit first goes to the data and metrics system, and then to the internal project management system, a powerful tool built on the data and metrics.

Amazon also has business review meetings, but with two key differences from most traditional companies. One is cadence: Amazon's review is on a weekly or bi-weekly basis. With the accelerated feedback and adjustment loop, Amazon can identify issues, and make mid-course adjustments much faster and with much more agility than its competitors.

The other is focus. Instead of focusing on historical performance and having each executive or manager do lengthy presentations, Amazon's review focuses more on how to solve particular customer problems and how to design and implement experimentations to improve, innovate, and invent.

In this sense, Amazon's data and metrics system liberates the executives from having to bury themselves in the routine day-to-day operations, and frees up more time and energy for them to devote to continuous improvement, innovation and invention, and to live in the future.

This is one of the pivot foundations for Bezos' vision of building Amazon into an invention machine.

THE FRONTLINE PEOPLE

In most traditional companies, once a decision is made by the boss, it is very hard to have it overturned. The inevitable waves of distortion and delays invariably compound the folly of the original decision, which, by the time the consequences are felt by frontline workers, feels completely off the rails.

When the frontline people receive such suboptimal or even "insane" instruction from a certain boss who is already detached and disconnected from current market dynamics, and current preferences of the target customers, what to do? In most cases, their only option is to suck it up and live with it.

Frontline people rarely have an opportunity to voice their views, let alone occupy a seat at the table when key decisions are being made. Even if they are lucky enough to be granted access, their views are invariably crushed by the boss, who behaves as if having more power and more experience somehow confers upon him more wisdom or customer experience.

At Amazon, the frontline people can be liberated from such painful frustrations. When difficult decisions are to be considered, frontline workers are encouraged (in fact required) to take the initiative of pulling all relevant data from the system and running the required analysis on their own. If the results support their views, there is no need to wait or to worry. They are expected to go to the boss immediately and get the flawed decisions in question reversed.

Also, given the transparency of data and metrics, frontline people don't have to wait for the boss' probing, questioning, and subsequent instructions weeks or months afterwards. When real-time data send the warning signals, the respective metric owner will take the immediate initiative on their own to identify root causes and develop corrective actions for mid-course adjustments.

Moreover, transparency of such ultra-detailed, end-to-end (cross-silo and cross-layer), real-time and inputs-oriented data and metrics makes the usual uphill battle for cross-functional collaboration much easier. Real-time data is the best persuasion point to get the right help from almost anyone in the company.

This is one of Amazon's secret ingredients for speed and agility.

THE CONTINUOUS BAR-RAISING

Almost all companies espouse a goal of a performance-driven culture. Without the strong support of a superbly robust data and metrics system, executives are often missing critical data they can use to make effective and informed decisions. In the absence of the most informative data, such aspirations do not fulfill their potential.

When Jeff Wilke joined Amazon in 1999 with the mission to fix the company's operations, one of his first changes he made was to devise "dozens of metrics" and order "his general managers to track them carefully, including how many shipments each fulfillment center received, how many orders were shipped out, and the per-unit cost of packing and shipping each item."[8]

Most people may think these are mundane tasks, but they're essential for customer convenience, operational excellence, and continuous bar-raising.

In fact this rigorous work proved itself to be instrumental to Amazon's future success in Prime (two-day free shipping for prime members) and FBA (Fulfillment by Amazon). Even today, twenty years later, one Chinese e-commerce mega-giant still struggles with how to get an accurate per-unit cost of packing and shipping for each item, and how to help general managers of fulfillment and dispatch centers improve performance.

That's why Wilke could promise Bezos "that he would reliably generate cost savings each year just by reducing defects and increasing productivity."[9] Of course, he also delivered. As you know, this is very important at Amazon.

Bezos always aspires to build a forever-Day-1 organization at Amazon. Continuous bar-raising is at the heart of this vision. The data and metrics system are in fact a foundational enabler to nail it down for everyone in every activity at Amazon in a crystal-clear, super-specific and highly measurable way.

THE AI-POWERED TOOLS

Before founding Amazon, Bezos worked for four years at D. E. Shaw and Co, a boutique investment firm on Wall Street, which actually let computers make all trading decisions.

During his weekly brainstorming session with founder David Shaw, Bezos was able to test out some earliest thoughts about the promise of the coming digital economy: he had already envisioned that some of Amazon's greatest inventions that have become the common practices we take for granted today, such as the ultimate personalization that treats each customer differently.

In the beginning of his 2010 Shareholder Letter, Bezos wrote:

> *"Random forests, naïve Bayesian estimators, RESTful services, gossip protocols, eventual consistency, data sharding, anti-entropy, Byzantine quorum, erasure coding, vector clocks .... walk into certain Amazon meetings, and you may momentarily think you've stumbled into a computer science lecture.*
>
> *"Look inside a current textbook on software architecture, and you'll find few patterns that we don't apply at Amazon. We use high-performance transactions systems, complex rendering and object caching, workflow and queuing systems, business intelligence and data analytics, machine learning and pattern recognition, neural networks and probabilistic decision making, and a wide variety of other techniques. And while many of our systems are based on the latest in computer science research, this often hasn't been sufficient: our architects and engineers have had to advance research in directions that no academic had yet taken. Many of the problems we*

face have no textbook solutions, and so we — happily — invent new approaches."

Clearly, Bezos' personal passion for technology and signature spirit of imagining and inventing has become one of Amazon's underlying characteristics. In this aspect, Amazon is the front-runner.

This is a key differentiator. How many CEOs and senior executives even have a feel of what these digital tools are and what magic these tools can do? If they don't have the feel personally, do they have someone who they can trust and who know how to apply these digital tools into business?

THE EXAMPLES

The applications of this approach are countless, and inform virtually all key decisions made by Amazon.

How does Amazon pick the location of its next fulfillment center? The answer is Mechanical Sensei, a software system "that simulated all the orders coursing through Amazon's fulfillment centers and predicted where new FCs would most productively be located."[10]

How does Amazon help the hundreds of thousands of third-party sellers who contributed $160Bn gross merchandise sales in 2018? By providing "the very best selling tools we could imagine and build."[11] Such tools help sellers incorporate all factors related to business operations, such as seasonality, historical results, future predictions, competitive offerings, and cash flow considerations, in order to make the best decisions in order, inventory, pricing and promotion, as well as provide the most convenient services in order processing, payment collection, shipment tracking and performance analysis.

How does Amazon manage the large number of third-party sellers, mostly small- and medium-businesses? From the very beginning, Amazon's third-party platform was developed based on the design principle of self-governance. The data and metrics system can meticulously track the performance of each third-party seller by using a whole set of metrics, and then roll the actual performance results along these metrics into an aggregated index score. For top performers, the system will automatically create various rewards according to the pre-defined rules specified in the algorithms; for the ones with issues, alerts will be sent and in severe cases, the management team will be involved in discussions before removing them from the Amazon platform.

AUTOMATION ENABLED PRICING

How does Amazon ensure its competitiveness in pricing? Pricing bots. These are "automated programs that crawled the Web, spied on competitors' prices, and then adjusted Amazon's prices accordingly, ensuring that Bezos's adamant demand that the company always match the lowest price anywhere, offline or online, would be met."[12]

How does Amazon drive more consumption from each consumer? Personalized recommendations. And who at Amazon decides which items to recommend to which customers? Actually . . . .no one. An algorithm-enabled system fully automates personalized recommendations for each individual consumer.

How does Amazon develop options and decide the fastest and cheapest delivery option for each order? By the early 2000s, an Amazon fulfillment software system could run millions of such decisions every hour. Given Amazon's relentless pursuit of improvement, its highly sophisticated fulfillment software systems have been on a never-ending treadmill of iterations ever since creation. In 2014 alone, Amazon "rolled out 280 major software improvements across the FC (fulfillment center) network. Our goal is to continue to iterate and improve on the design, layout, technology, and operations in these buildings, ensuring that each new facility we build is better than the last."[13]

* * * * * * * *

Enabled by the two foundational building blocks, meaning the right people (Building Block 2) and the right data, metrics and AI-powered tools (Building Block 3), Amazon is now well set for a long-thought-to-be-impossible mission: building a continuous and accelerating invention machine aimed generating ground-breaking, game-changing and customer behavior-shaping inventions that create new market spaces and economic opportunities of massive magnitude.

It sounds highly intriguing, but also really seems impossible. We are with you. So how to make invention Amazon's DNA? How to construct an invention machine up to such high aspirations?

We welcome you to the next chapter.

REFLECTIONS AND IDEAS TO CONSIDER FOR YOUR COMPANY

CHAPTER HIGHLIGHTS

BUILDING BLOCK 4

Amazon's invention machine is continuous, accelerating, and aimed at generating ground-breaking, game-changing and customer behavior-shaping inventions that create new market spaces and economic opportunities of massive magnitude.

RELENTLESS DRIVE TO INVENT

Daring to learn new skills
Daring to kill own business
Daring to fail, in a big way
Daring to be patient

SEEK BIG IDEAS CONTINUOUSLY

Seek ideas from everyone
Must be big, really big
Must invent on behalf of customers
Must be distinctively differentiated

BUILD THE IDEA PATIENTLY

Who are the customers?
What are the goals?
What are the hurdles?

CONSTRUCT THE TEAM CAREFULLY

Build a total-immersion team
Pick the right team leader
Enforce end-to-end accountability

BUILDING BLOCK 4:

GROUND-BREAKING INVENTION MACHINE

What makes Amazon an outlier above all others is the sheer power of its identify as an invention machine: one that is able to deliver continuously, and at an ever-accelerating pace, ground-breaking, game-changing, and customer behavior-shaping inventions that create new market spaces and economic opportunities of massive magnitude.

That's probably why Fortune Magazine described Bezos as "the ultimate disruptor" in 2012, Fast Company Magazine named Amazon the world's most innovative company in 2017, and Forbes put Amazon on its list of World's Most Innovative Companies in 2018.

Amazon's scientists are leaders in their fields, from machine learning to computational linguistics. Amazon geeks out on some of the coolest science in the world. In a 2018 feature on Amazon's dayone blog, readers could find out about how:

- Amazon is sponsoring the second annual Widening Natural-Language Processing workshop, whose goal is to support women and underrepresented minorities working in the increasingly popular field of natural-language processing (NLP). "Two Amazon scientists — Lucie Flekova and Amittai Axelrod — were on the organizing committee, which was led by Princeton postdoc Libby Barak and also included Carnegie Mellon's Diyi Yang and the University of Sheffield's Zeerak Waseem,"the blog reported. Amazon has undertaken a number of initiatives to support the education and development of women and minorities in computer science.

- University teams worldwide are competing for the $3.5 million pool of prizes and grants through the Amazon Alexa Prize by developing a socialbot that can converse coherently and engagingly with humans.
- Amazon and chief machine learning scientist Bernhard Schölkopf, is deeply engaged in the 2018 NeurIPS Conference where Amazon is sharing insights and applying advances in Bayesian learning, spiking neural networks, and chit-chat based and social bots.
- Dilek Hakkani-Tür, a senior principal scientist in the Alexa AI group, is seeing "a lot of advancements in image processing and speech and in many machine learning problems. Within dialogue, it's still so hard to have machines that can learn how to converse in an open domain. I think that's why people want to work on the problem." Learn more at https://blog.aboutamazon.com/amazon-ai/the-state-of-ai.

This all flows from how much Bezos loves invention, which is clearly embedded in his DNA. His flair for invention showed up early in his childhood. His grandpa would assist him in "an open umbrella spine clad in aluminum foil for a solar cooking experiment; an ancient Hoover vacuum cleaner being transformed into a primitive hovercraft."[1]

As founder and CEO of Amazon, Bezos wants to inject this invention DNA into Amazon, the company he created. In addition to sustaining the relentless drive to invent, Bezos also wants Amazon to master the necessary skills and the effective methodologies for invention.

Again this is no piece of cake. Most people would probably find this task too daunting to even try. But for Bezos, a born inventor and builder, the "impossible" challenge simply kindles more fire within.

"We want to be a large company that's also an invention machine."[2] (Our emphasis).

RELENTLESS DRIVE TO INVENT

Invention is not an everyday task that fits everyone. Not everyone has the relentless drive needed. Most of those who are attracted by these impressive returns haven't fully grasped that such returns invariably come with a hefty price tag: the costs of invention. They will talk a lot about innovation and sincerely aspire for invention, but have neither invested enough effort to figure out the innate costs associated with ground-breaking inventions nor made the conscious choice to accept these costs. When faced with these costs, they want to avoid them as much as possible.

What they fail to see is that costs and returns are two sides of the same coin. Rejecting the costs actually suffocates invention in its true sense, and by doing so, they are actually setting themselves up for failure.

So what are the innate costs associated with ground-breaking inventions? Let's spend some quality time together on learning about them and thinking about the conscious choice required for serious commitment to inventions.

DARING TO LEARN NEW SKILLS

In a 2009 Fast Company interview, Bezos said, "There are two ways to extend a business. Take inventory of what you're good at and extend out from your skills," that is the well-known concept of core competencies, or "determine what your customers need and work backward, even if it requires learning new skills."

Most companies that have built thriving enterprises eventually evolve into a more protective and defensive mindset in which they cling dearly onto its core competencies accumulated from the past; and seek to preserve and maximize short-term gains without investing enough in learning new skills required for the future. In this way, Motorola let Nokia take the lead, and ironically in the same way, Nokia passed the lead to Apple.

Since the first day Bezos has always focused clearly on serving future customer needs, and has been willing to work backwards to learn the new skills required. In fact, in a 2008 interview with Business Week, Bezos made the point that companies that innovate within their existing competencies are doomed to fail; innovation means building new competencies.[3]

This has been the common theme of Amazon's invention and innovation. Just think about the impressive list of major breakthroughs in the company's history, such as AWS, Kindle, and Alexa and Echo. When Amazon first started, none of the cloud, hardware, voice recognition, or AI was among the portfolio of existing competencies at that time.

Perhaps a little less obvious: the continuous learning of new skills generates compounding returns over time. The more new skills developed, the more new opportunities will be created and captured; and as such new opportunities unfold, the better the skills will be, and the higher the returns will be.

For example, when in 2004, Bezos decided to pursue a crazy idea that later became Kindle, Amazon had zero experience in hardware devices. When Amazon first ventured into the unchartered waters that later became AWS, nobody knew for sure what would be the outcome. With fast learning and proven mastery in both device and cloud-based services, Amazon's later adventure of Echo seemed to be much more well-grounded.

This is what we meant by "compounding effects of inventions."

DARING TO KILL OWN BUSINESS

In the case of Kindle, Amazon not only had the courage back in 2004 to get into the most crowded and competitive market of consumer electronics, but also didn't shy away from the risk of self-cannibalization.

This threat was very real at the time. Amazon had made its first success in selling physical books online. If Kindle could do what it promised, customers could easily find and download an e-book within 60 seconds, without the trouble of buying or carrying physical books.

The extreme success of Kindle could put all sellers of physical books out of business, including Amazon itself.

That's why when Bezos appointed Steve Kessel, then a key executive in the traditional media business (including the selling of physical books), to lead Kindle and transition to digital media, he explicitly told Kessel "Your job is to kill your own business. I want you to proceed as if your goal is to put everyone selling physical books out of a job."[4] Amazon was clearly one of the "everyone" selling physical books.

When given this appointment, Kessel's previous job, with all its responsibilities and subordinates, was immediately taken away from him. Why not allow Kessel to manage both the physical and digital media business at the same time? The answer was crystal clear to Bezos, "If you are running both businesses, you will never go after the digital opportunity with tenacity."[5]

Bezos' approach could leave many puzzled. Why was he so determined? Because Bezos knows too well that if you don't dare to kill your own business, others will. The classic example would be Kodak, who used to be the unequivocal global leader in the film market but filed for bankruptcy in 2012. The interesting part is that Kodak in fact invented the digital camera.

DARING TO FAIL, IN A BIG WAY

Failure is a necessary and integral part of invention. There is no shortcut here. To pursue invention, tolerance of failure is a must. Or more precisely, the possibility of failure should be encouraged and embraced.

Amazon clearly understands this point and actually believes in failing early and iterating until they get it right. Such a belief gives Amazons a distinctive competitive edge, and frees Amazon to "pioneer into the unexplored spaces."[6] As Bezos explained:

"One area where I think we are especially distinctive is failure. I believe we are the best place in the world to fail (we have plenty of practice!), and failure and invention are inseparable twins.[19] To invent you have to experiment, and if you know in advance that it's going to work, it's not an experiment."[7]

During the past 25 years of innovation and invention, Amazon has encountered numerous failures. Here are the 18 significant ones:[8]

Year	Failed Innovations (year abandoned, if applicable)
1999	1. Amazon Auctions (abandoned 2000) 2. zShop (abandoned 2007)
2004	3. A9 search portal (abandoned 2008)
2006	4. Askville (abandoned 2013) 5. Unbox (abandoned 2015)
2007	6. Endless.com (abandoned 2012) 7. Amazon WedPay (abandoned 2014)
2009	8. PayPhrase (abandoned 2012)
2010	9. Webstore (abandoned 2016)
2011	10. MyHabit (abandoned 2016) 11. Amazon Local (abandoned 2015) 12. Test Drive (abandoned 2015)
2012	13. Music Importer (abandoned 2015)
2014	14. Fire Phone (abandoned 2015) 15. Amazon Elements diapers (abandoned 2015) 16. Amazon Local Register (abandoned 2015) 17. Amazon Wallet (abandoned 2015)
2015	18. Amazon Destinations (abandoned 2015)

Interestingly, as a company grows bigger, if one wants to continue to invent at a size that can move the needle, the experiment needs to be big enough to really matter. Since it's an experiment, no one can guarantee success; the size of failed experiments will go up as well. As a result, unless you can **make peace with the possibility of large-scale failure** (large-scale risk-taking implied), large-scale success will not come. That's why Bezos mentioned the phrase, "multibillion-dollar failures," for the first time, in his 2018 Shareholder Letter.

Among the 18 failures mentioned above, the Fire Phone is undeniably a multibillion-dollar failure. However, from the ashes of Fire phone,

Amazon was able to harvest its learnings and leverage the experience of its developers to accelerate Echo and Alexa. Those two proved to be victories that turned out to be much larger in scale and much longer in timeframe.

Bezos is not alone in such daring to fail. In June 2017, Netflix CEO Reed Hastings told a technology conference, "Our hit ratio is too high right now. We have to take more risks . . . . to try more crazy things . . . . we should have a higher cancel rate overall."[9]

DARING TO BE PATIENT

Invention is anything but efficient. It's difficult, lengthy, and full of uncertainty because no one knows how much longer it will take and when the real breakthrough is going to come.

To copy, to follow conventional wisdom or to benchmark against best practices would be much easier, much faster, much more certain and efficient.

Bezos is well aware of the difference between the two approaches and fully appreciates the beauty of the former's inefficiency. In his words, this is power of "wandering," clearly not efficient, but definitely required for invention, especially for the "outsized discoveries, the 'non-linear' ones."[10]

It takes patience to wait, sometimes for years. It also takes courage to shrug off the long periods of misunderstanding for years. All of Amazon's ground-breaking, game-changing, and customer behavior-shaping inventions has taken years to develop: two years for AWS to launch its first service, three years for Kindle from development to product debut, four years and a 2000-member team for Echo, and "several years building our own data engine, Amazon Aurora, a fully-managed MySQL and PostgreSQL-compatible service with the same or better durability and availability as the commercial engines, but at one-tenth of the cost."[11]

SEEK BIG IDEAS CONTINUOUSLY

All great inventions need to start with an idea, a brilliant one, a revolutionary one, or a seemingly impossible one. So how does Amazon continuously generate new ideas and meticulously pick which ones to pursue?

SEEK IDEAS FROM EVERYONE

Many people have great inspirations. However, much of this potential brilliance is wasted as a result of the "omission bias," an interesting phenomenon highlighted by Patrick Doyle, CEO of Domino's Pizza since 2010. That is "the reality that most people with a new idea choose not to pursue the idea because if they try something and it doesn't work, the setback might damage their career."[12]

How to overcome this barrier and ensure that people with the new ideas, the great ideas, and the seemingly crazy ideas have both the courage and the channel to voice their views and be heard without fear?

Amazon invented a unique way, called "the idea tool," to tap into employees' creativity and imagination. Anyone who has an idea can submit his or her thoughts without filters of layers of managers or concerns about feasibility from either technical or financial points of view.

For example, the initial idea, which later developed into "Prime," was in fact a proposal made by an Amazon junior software engineer called Charlie Ward back in 2004. His thought that Amazon could "offer people kind of an all-you-can-eat buffet of fast, free delivery."[13] By that fall, this idea had gathered enthusiasm among other employees and caught Bezos' attention. Immediately hooked by this "big idea," Bezos called for a Saturday meeting nearby his home and kicked off the destiny-defining journey for Amazon right on the spot. As of year-end 2018, Amazon has more than 100 million prime members worldwide,[14] the second-highest number of paid subscribers only next to Netflix.[15]

In addition to the people inside Amazon, Bezos also seeks ideas from those outside. After the initial success of selling books over the Internet, Bezos "emailed a thousand randomly selected customers and asked them, besides the things we sell today, what would you like to see us sell."[16]

Once you have the ideas, how to select which one to pursue further?

MUST BE BIG, REALLY BIG

At Amazon, the ideal adventure to create is not aimed at merely 100 or 1000 people. Bezos seeks inventions that speak to billions of customers and millions of enterprises worldwide. With Internet and digital technology, this is both feasible and economically attractive. The $232.9Bn revenue[17] a year is still very small. All in all, Amazon only commands less than 4% of US retail and less than 1% of global retail.[18]

In his 2017 interview with Fast Company, Bezos said, "Our job is to provide a great customer experience, and that is something that's universally desired all over the world." Why universally? Why all over the world? Because that's about the scale Bezos has in mind.

Why so big? Because of the risky nature of invention, in which "failure and invention are inseparable twins." What could offset the numerous failures along the way? A big win, such as AWS.

Other than a large addressable customer base, what else could ensure big scale? The answer is "simple." Steve Jobs firmly believed that the best design is the simplest. On this point, Bezos couldn't agree more. "Simple is the key to easy, fast, intuitive, and low-cost." More importantly, "simple scales much better than complex."[20] (Our emphasis).

That's why Amazon's third Leadership Principle, right after Customer Obsession and Ownership, is "Invent and Simplify."

No wonder the first service launched by AWS back in 2006 was Simple Storage Service, and during the entire development process, Bezos constantly reminded the team to simplify further.

MUST INVENT ON BEHALF OF CUSTOMERS

Amazon famously obsesses with customers because they are "divinely discontent." As Bezos wrote, "People have a voracious appetite for a better way, and yesterday's 'wow' quickly becomes today's 'ordinary.'"[21]

Amazon also chooses to focus on customers instead of competitors because, "If you're competitor-focused, you have to wait until there is a competitor doing something.... Being customer-focused allows you to be more pioneering."[22]

By focusing on customers and their discontents, you will open up the floodgates of never-ending inspirations. Once truly obsessed with how to continuously delight them you will be surprised at how many ideas you could come up with.

Regarding customers, Bezos has a very high bar. What he looks for is an experience that dramatically exceeds customers' expectations, something that has been long believed impossible, and something that would generate a genuine "wow" or even a "magic" moment.

In other words, Amazon invents on behalf of customers, instead of waiting for customers to say what they want.

> *"The biggest needle movers in Amazon are exact things that customers don't know to ask for. We must invent on their behalf. We have to tap into our own inner imagination about what's possible. AWS itself – as a whole – is an example.[23]"*

MUST BE DISTINCTIVELY DIFFERENTIATED

To constantly delight and wow customers, the idea has to be distinctively differentiated from others. It is even better to be unique, or seemingly impossible. Bezos has no interest in being a copycat or offering a me-too product or service. Before embarking on an idea, he ensures that it is actually worth doing, "we want something that's uniquely Amazon.[24]" (Our emphasis).

Bezos therefore strongly encourages his team to always imagine the impossible. Amazon Go is the perfect example. Bezos had been asked for years whether Amazon would open physical stores and his reply had always been "yes" but only when Amazon could come up with something different. This day finally came with Amazon Go. This venture called for a complete re-imagination of a whole new customer experience: walking into a store, picking up what is needed and just walking out without "annoying and lasting-for-ever checkout lines" anymore.[25] Many customers describe the experience of shopping at Amazon Go as "magical".[26]

That's exactly what Amazon looks for in great ideas.

BUILD THE IDEA PATIENTLY

In many companies, once an idea has successfully attracted the attention and support of one top executive or the CEO, implying the approval of team and budget, it's time for rubber to hit the road.

The Amazon way is radically different. It all starts with the press release. This formal exercise enables people to further ponder and polish the idea, to make it more robust and more specific, and to develop this big idea from a simple concept to a development-ready blueprint. It is an internal document that looks at what the future would be like with the successful execution of the idea being proposed.

According to John Rossman, a former Amazon executive, a sample press release for the third-party selling platform would go as follows:

"Amazon Announces Huge Growth in Third-Party Selling, Delighting Customers and Sellers

Seattle, WA: Amazon announced results for the third-party selling business today. Using the third-party selling platform, Amazon customers can now shop across many categories of products today including apparel, sporting goods, home decor, jewelry and electronics with incredible selection, price and an experience equaling orders fulfilled by Amazon.

The Amazon customer now thinks about Amazon for any retail need, thanks to the third-party selling business. Over 30% of all orders at Amazon are now third-party sold and fulfilled orders, across 10 new and expanded product categories," explained Director of Merchant Integration John Rossman. "We tackled several difficult hurdles to make this successful, with the key being that sellers had a great experience. Sellers can now register, list products to sell, take orders and fulfill in the middle of the night, without ever having to talk to someone at Amazon." [27]

From this 142-word document, one can clearly see 3 things that would play pivotal roles in the following development:

WHO ARE THE CUSTOMERS?

At Amazon, every project, be it development, innovation, or invention, needs to start with the customer.

Potential questions to answer include: Who are the customers? How will they use it? What is their new experience? Which existing experience will it replace? What changes will it require them to make? Why will they prefer it? What are the benefits in the eyes of the customers? If the customers are not the end users, you need to go all the way to the end users and think through the same set of questions again.

Amazon always considers customer experience as an end-to-end process. Each touch point along the customer journey matters, regardless of whether it is under your control or not. Customers don't care who owns which part of the process, whose KPIs it is, or whose role and responsibility. If they don't like the experience, they will go somewhere else. Therefore, the end user experiences need to be equally great no matter which party—third-party sellers or first-party seller (i.e. Amazon itself)—provides the service.

WHAT ARE THE GOALS?

Given the innate uncertainty of product development, many companies take a "wait and see" approach towards setting goals. At Amazon, goals are taken seriously. They need to be bold, specific, and measurable.

Goals cannot be a low-hanging fruit that one can achieve easily. They must be so high up in the sky that they are almost beyond the eyesight of many and can only be achieved through audacious effort. What drives creativity? It's the challenges. If something gets too easy, people's true creativity will be left under-utilized or even un-tapped.

Back in the early days, Amazon had been struggling with third-party sales. Total percentage of third-party selling was a stagnant three percent in 1999 and 2000. Amazon Auctions and zShop, two attempts to conquer the third-party arena launched in 1999 both failed. Despite all these setbacks, the team for the third-party selling platform set their goal at thirty percent, implying a 10-time jump.

At Amazon, before the kick-off of any new product or service project, the team must set a specific launch date in the press release. This is not a firm commitment that can trigger firing or other punishment if the owners of the idea fail to launch on that date. Rather, the discipline of putting one's best guess on the table — and in formal writing — has tremendous value as a strong forcing mechanism for thinking things through thoroughly, taking one's proposal seriously and, when faced with difficulty, pushing oneself to do everything humanly possible to honor one's own commitment.

Prime is an excellent example. When Bezos decided to kick off the project, he set the launch date at the next earnings announcement, leaving the team only eight weeks to turn the huge idea into a ready-to-launch flawless solution.

All these goals are bold, specific, and thus measurable. In this way, there is no wiggle room to tweak a lukewarm result into a glamorous hit or to paint a failure into glory.

WHAT ARE THE HURDLES?

To convert a big idea — one that is distinctively differentiated, uniquely Amazon, and even seemingly impossible — into reality is never easy. After all, there must be almost insurmountable hurdles that prevent others from trying or even imagining the possibility of success.

In the case of the third-party selling platform, one huge initial hurdle was how to make it mostly self-service and automated. Why did the team choose this design principle despite all the difficulties? Because these qualities would maximize its ability to scale, so it could be big, really big.

This is also why the enabling and the governing of third-party sellers needs to be automated as well.

Most people would assume that the easiest way to help third-party sellers operate their business better and grow their business faster would be to conduct training or offer specific help via experienced veterans through calls, on-site visits, or coaching and consulting. That's not the best approach under this design principle, so the team wouldn't even stray there.

This is exactly the value that a well-thought-out press release would offer: clarity and discipline.

As you would well expect that writing a solid press release requires long time of in-depth thinking. Sometimes, it can take ten or more iterations.

CONSTRUCT THE TEAM CAREFULLY

After the press release has been shared and discussed, and the big idea developed from a simple concept to a development-ready blueprint, it's time to select a leader and put together a team to make it happen.

Amazon has a well-known approach to drive project development: the two-pizza team, or as Amazon refers to it, 2PT. The 2PT teams refer to "autonomous groups of fewer than ten people — small enough that, when working late, the team members could be fed with two pizza pies."[28]

Many people take the concept literally, i.e., the team size, usually 6-10 people. As Bezos repeatedly pointed out, if you can't feed a team with two pizzas, the team is probably too big.

Is team size the only thing that matters? Of course not.

BUILD A TOTAL-IMMERSION TEAM

At Amazon, a project team with clear mission and specific goals needs to be cross-functional, full-time, and co-located. It's a total immersion experience with the team constantly working together, hour upon hour, days and nights, and in some cases, months and years.

Why? Creativity comes from people's interactions; inspiration comes from intensive concentration. Just like a start-up, the initial founding team huddles together in a garage, experimenting, iterating, discussing, debating, trying and retrying, again and again. One idea triggers another, one inspiration sparks another, and eventually a destiny-defining breakthrough comes.

Many companies that want to adopt the 2PT approach indeed set up teams with 6-10 people, but usually fail to make them cross-functional, full-time, and co-located. When all team members have their respective full-time jobs to work on and various sets of demanding KPIs to deliver, their participation in the project, no matter how critical it is, is bounded to be reduced to something more like extra-curricular activities for one or two random hours every week. They have no choice but to opt out of weekly team meetings if duty calls. That's why full attendance at team meetings is so rare. In most cases, even when they do show up, their minds are somewhere else.

In short, the projects may well be the top priorities for the company, but full-time dedication and co-located concentration, the individuals never see them that way.

PICK THE RIGHT TEAM LEADER

The right leader may not guarantee success, but the wrong leader will surely guarantee failure. In each of Amazon's major breakthroughs, you will find a strong leader.

Back in 1999, who led the Amazon logistics, and built fulfillment into a core competency? Jeff Wilke. He is now the CEO of Worldwide Consumer. In fact, Fulfillment by Amazon (FBA) has become an important enabling infrastructure for Amazon ecosystem partners.

Who led the mission to create Kindle and was full-heartedly devoted to the courageous and audacious endeavor into the unknown, even when it meant "killing your own business?" Steve Kessel. He is now the SVP of physical stores.

Who led the invention of cloud services and built AWS into a $26.7Bn revenue business?[29] Andy Jassy. He is now the CEO of AWS.

All the three are currently S-team members led by Bezos personally.

Nothing overcomes the wrong person. In the wrong hands, great ideas will not blossom.

ENFORCE END-TO-END ACCOUNTABILITY

In most companies, when things go south, finger-pointing becomes a routine charade.

For example, when a new product fails to deliver expected revenue and profits after three years' trying, the R and D team will be blamed by others for poor design, the sales team will be blamed for poor selling, and the product team will be blamed for poor judgement about market and poor understanding of customer needs. Some collateral damage will be inevitable during the crossfire.

At Amazon, the project team is held accountable end-to-end (e2e), meaning their ownership extends all the way from concept, to design, to development, to testing, to launch, and to post-launch operation.

Why? Bezos believes in the principle of "eat your own dog food." This is a forcing mechanism of enforcing crystal clear accountability for everyone with nowhere to hide, no one at whom to point the finger.

****

Bezos is clearly succeeding in building an invention machine at Amazon that is able to continuously generate ground-breaking, game-changing and customer behavior-shaping inventions that create new market spaces and economic opportunities of massive magnitude.

As Bezos proudly announced that "invention is our DNA"[30] and "inventions have become second nature at Amazon."[31]

However his job is far from done. Bezos needs to remain vigilant, constantly on guard against the subtle traps that could break this incredible invention machine. Among all possible traps, he singled out decision-making as particularly important.

> *"We want to be a large company that's also an invention machine .... Can we do it? I'm optimistic .... but I don't think it'll be easy. There are some subtle traps that even high-performing large organizations can fall into .... and we'll have to learn as an institution how to guard against them. One common pitfall for large organizations – one that hurts speed and inventiveness – is 'one-size-fits-all' decision making."*[32]

Lengthy decision-making coupled with layers of endless approval processes can wear down a fighter, extinguish a creative fire and dampen the passion for invention. Fully aware of the stakes at hand, how would Amazon design a decision-making mechanism to fix the "one-size-fits-all" problem?

Let's explore this in the next chapter: High-Velocity and High-Quality Decision-Making.

REFLECTIONS AND IDEAS TO CONSIDER FOR YOUR COMPANY

BUILDING BLOCK 5:
HIGH-VELOCITY AND HIGH-QUALITY DECISION-MAKING

Amazon's decision-making is high-velocity, high-quality, and strictly follows a set of clearly articulated principles and uniquely designed methodology enforced with striking consistency throughout the organization.

TYPE 2 DECISIONS: SPEED MATTERS

Don't do one-size-fits-all
Don't make all decisions yourself
Don't wait for all the information
Let the metrics owner make the call
From sequential to parallel approval
Digitize math-based routine decisions

TYPE 1 DECISIONS: FOCUS ON A FEW

Find the best truth
Imagine the possible change
Combat group thinking
Have backbone; disagree and commit
Minimize regrets
What if a decision goes wrong?

SCALE UP GOOD DECISION-MAKING

Crystalize consistent principles
Specify consistent methodology: narratives
Enforce consistent approach in every decision

BUILDING BLOCK 5:

HIGH-VELOCITY AND HIGH-QUALITY DECISION-MAKING

In most pre-digital companies, decision-making is slow. All readers probably know well about it out of your own experience.

In the traditional setup, only very few people at the top of the hierarchy, usually CEO, CFO, and the head of strategy, know the full picture and are thus capable of making a right choice with all of the right factors taken into consideration. As a result, such bureaucratic decision-making, featured by lengthy layers of approvals, intensive politics among silos, extensive gaming-of-the-system by all, and lack of transparency of data (especially lacking customer data as driving element of decision-making), is not only low in velocity, but also could be low in quality.

These processes make their own kind of sense as they are essentially designed for command and control, not for speed and agility as in the case of their digital counterparties.

What's more: Amazon's decision-making is not only high in both velocity and quality, but also high in scale, with a set of clearly articulated principles and a uniquely designed methodology enforced with striking consistency throughout the organization.

How can Amazon upgrade its decision-making and achieve the three seemingly conflicting goals of speed, quality, and scale at the same time?

TYPE 2 DECISIONS: SPEED MATTERS

Bezos established speed as the top priority, both for himself and senior executives. "The senior team at Amazon is determined to keep our decision-making velocity high."[1] How to do it?

DON'T DO ONE-SIZE-FITS-ALL

Bezos categorized all decisions into two types and designed different kinds of decision-making processes depending on whether they were a Type 1 or Type 2 decision.

Type 1 decisions refer to those that "are consequential and irreversible or nearly irreversible – one-way doors . . . . If you walk through and don't like what you see on the other side, you can't get back to where you were before."[2]

Because of the long-term implications, Bezos suggested that Type 1 decisions should go through a heavy-weight process to ensure they are of high quality. "These decisions must be made methodically, carefully, slowly, with great deliberation and consultation."[3]

However, most decisions aren't like that.

Type 2 decisions refer to those that "are changeable, reversible – they're two-way doors. If you've made a suboptimal Type 2 decision, you don't have to live with the consequences for that long. You can reopen the door and go back through."[4]

The distinction between these two types of decisions and the different types of decision-making mechanisms associated with each must be crystal clear. Applying the heavy-weight process on Type 2 decisions will lead to slowness, risk aversion, failure to experiment sufficiently, and diminished invention. At the same time, taking Type 1 decisions lightly is a huge mistake: one fatal mistake in Type 1 decisions could lead to extinction.

DON'T MAKE ALL DECISIONS YOURSELF

As CEO, you should identify and delegate the Type 2 decisions, as they "can and should be made quickly by high judgment individuals or small groups."[5]

No matter how hard-working you and your top team are, everyone only has 24 hours a day. Assume that if your business continues to grow, and decision-making is still concentrated at the top, sooner or later, you will become the biggest bottleneck for fast growth.

Of course, you need to give careful thought to whom to delegate, and how to make the designated individual or the small group successful. Pulling several relevant people together into a standing committee, as many traditional companies do, without necessary support in right data in the right format, clear accountability or timely coaching, will not end well.

DON'T WAIT FOR ALL THE INFORMATION

In war, when timing is even more critical, former U.S. Secretary of State and retired four-star general Colin Powell advocated a 40-70 Rule: if you have less than 40% of the information, you shouldn't make a decision. But if you wait until you have more than 70% of the information, you have waited too long. Once the information is in the 40-70 range, go with your gut.[6]

In business, Bezos used a 70-90 rule instead. He stated that "most decisions should probably be made with somewhere around 70% of the information you wish you had. If you wait for 90%, in most cases, you're probably being slow. Plus, either way, you need to be good at quickly recognizing and correcting bad decisions. If you're good at course correcting, being wrong may be less costly than you think, whereas being slow is going to be expensive for sure."[7]

In fact, Amazon enjoys a huge built-in advantage in this way. Amazon's real-time data transparency and anomaly detection enabled by its AI-powered data and metrics becomes extremely helpful.

LET THE METRICS OWNER MAKE THE CALL

At Amazon, each operation has a set of metrics to ensure operational excellence, and each metrics has one designated metrics owner.

In this way, the metrics owner is the single point of accountability, so no more finger-pointing; the owner has full access to all the relevant data and analytics, so no more being handicapped by partial information; and the owner has clear authorization to take corrective initiatives, with maximum one-level of approval, so no more heavy-weight decision-making.

If cross-functional collaboration is required, the metric owner is both obliged and empowered to convince others using data analytics. If experimentation is required when facing the unknown, the metric owner can run low-cost fast-feedback pilots using data analytics. If mid-course correction is required, the metric owner can solicit valuable inputs and gain approvals from others during weekly review, again using data analytics.

In short, such data transparency, clear accountability, and liberating authorization empower the metrics owner to identify glitches faster, get to the bottom of the root causes faster, and take the corrective actions faster.

This is of crucial importance to the speed and agility required in the digital age. More importantly, this is impossible without the right people (Building Block 2) who are equipped with the right AI-powered data and metrics system (Building Block 3).

FROM SEQUENTIAL TO PARALLEL APPROVAL

High-velocity decision-making does not mean getting rid of necessary gatekeepers.

For Type 2 decisions, when multiple functions need to be involved in approval, you can transform the traditional sequential process into a parallel operation for high-velocity decision-making.

For example, at Amazon, project teams are free to choose between internal services and external vendors. By the traditional sequential selection and approval process, this could take two to three months.

To ensure speed, Amazon forms a cross-functional team composed of people from procurement, technology, finance, legal and other required functions.

With such a team in place, the lengthy sequential approval process is replaced by an effective group discussion with all the available relevant facts, analyses and perspectives, effectively considered and efficiently decided.

For most cases, multi-function, multi-layer, multi-people involvement in the approval processes can prevent clear accountability. When one person is appointed to be accountable, decisions happen faster. For example, at Amazon, each project team is assigned a senior executive as project sponsor. One level approval from one single person always accelerates decision-making.

DIGITIZE MATH-BASED ROUTINE DECISIONS

Amazon's powerful data, metrics, and AI-powered tools, mean that many sophisticated but routine operational decisions that used to be handled only by long-term industry veterans with decades of experience and expertise, can now be digitized.

One typical example: how to manage inventory purchasing. The right balance needs to be found in managing conflicting needs of keeping enough in stock to ensure immediate availability to customers, and inventory turnover as high as possible, while at the same time, keeping the inventory level and inventory-associated costs as low as possible.

Given the availability of vast amounts of historical data about customer orders, seasonal volatility, and replenishment speed of vendors, and all the AI-powered analytics and prediction tools, this is a typical math-based routine decision that can be largely digitized.

In the same spirit, decisions such as location picking of the next fulfillment center have long been digitized, as we mentioned in the chapter of AI-Powered Data and Metrics System (Building Block 3).

TYPE 1 DECISIONS: FOCUS ON A FEW

While powerful digital tools can indeed free us from many routine mundane math-based decisions, not all decisions can be delegated or digitized.

What to do with the important Type 1 decisions? These few decisions, though small in absolute number, are one-way, consequential, and destiny-defining. Unlike the math-based routine decisions, these destiny-defining decisions are usually very controversial and inevitably end up in heated debates.

There are plenty of such examples in Amazon's 25-year history. In the cases of ground-breaking inventions, there is no precedent to follow, no luxury of solid historical data to analyze. There was no roadmap to follow, for example, when Bezos took the decision in 2004 to get into the cut-throat consumer electronics market with no hardware expertise; a decision which led to the invention of Kindle and accelerated Amazon's endeavor into Echo and Alexa.

For these tough Type 1 decisions, who should be held accountable?

To Bezos, the answer is crystal clear. He himself, as the founder and CEO of Amazon, is first and foremost the chief decision-making officer. In an interview last year, Bezos actually said, "As a senior executive, you get paid to make a small number of high-quality decisions. Your job is not to make thousands of decisions every day."[8]

Once accountability gets clarified, how to ensure high-quality and high-velocity for these decisions?

FIND THE BEST TRUTH

In many legacy organizations, due to the inevitable delay, distortion, and manipulation through layers of relayed information from bottom to the top, many decisions are made far from the truth, the whole truth, and nothing but the truth.

For example, in the Challenger disaster, Nobel laureate Richard Feynman revealed the simple truth via his famous C-clamp experiment, dropping a piece of the O-ring material squeezed with a C-clamp into ice water.[9] It showed that the rubber sealing could become frozen, brittle and easily breakable in cold temperature (31°F/-0.5°C) during the launch, something that had not been duly considered in the final decision-making process.

If this piece of critical information and the corresponding high likelihood of devastating results had been brought to the full attention of the final decision-makers, the tragedy might have been avoided.

As well documented in a 2013 HBR (Harvard Business Review) article, Bezos' right-handed man Rick Dalzell said, one of the two things that Bezos does better than anyone else is that "he tries to find the best truth at all the time."[10] This may sound too obvious to even be mentioned, but it is actually a big challenge for traditional organizations usually characterized by strict hierarchy, managing by fear, and a command and control modus operandi.

IMAGINE THE POSSIBLE CHANGE

In addition to the best truth in a static sense, Bezos takes it to one step further, i.e., always using future-back perspective, thinking about how things will change going forward.

For example, back in 2005, most Amazon executives opposed Bezos regarding the launch of Prime. Brad Stone actually used the word "almost alone" to describe the lonely fight Bezos had back then.

Their objection was well-founded. Given an eight dollar logistics cost per order, and assuming twenty orders a year on average by each Prime member, it would cost $160 a year in shipping — more than double the $79 membership fee. Amazon executive Diego Piacentini recalled, "Every single financial analysis said we were completely crazy to give two-day shipping for free."[11]

So what gave Bezos such unwavering conviction despite the siege from all sides?

The key factor we would like to explore here is logistics cost. As you see, most people think in a static and linear sense, so they would merely see that logistics cost is eight dollars per order.

But Bezos thinks in a different way. Unfettered by the status quo, he envisions the future and then works backwards to create a strategy to make it happen, by asking the obvious but commonly neglected question: **how will it change?**

Back then, Bezos firmly believed that logistics cost, just one of the many factors in play here, would drop and that when put in a holistic future perspective, prime would become profitable in the future.

Why? Because when customers spent more, Amazon's volume would increase, and the increased scale could help Amazon negotiate lower prices from shipping vendors, and decrease the amount of fixed-cost allocation on each shipment. In addition, with a continuous system upgrade, Amazon's logistics system would continue to "drive down Amazon's transportation costs by double-digit percentages each year."[12] Furthermore, more spending per customer and higher value per order would generate higher gross profits than what would be needed to cover the shipping costs.

In fact, Bezos has been proven right. Morgan Stanley research[13] found that, on average, Prime members spent 2.7-time higher than non-prime member, and Prime actually enjoyed nineteen percent order margin, after logistics costs deducted.

COMBAT GROUP THINKING

Bezos recognizes the built-in human weakness in decision-making, and the subsequent biases and misjudgments (regardless of how great the person is) so well that he places huge emphasis on fighting conformity, challenging group thinking, and resisting the overrated importance of harmony.

He expects people to challenge him. He clearly demands a quality discussion where people introduce new ideas, different perspectives, and, even better, disruptive thinking. He "believes that truth springs forth when ideas and perspectives are banged against each other, sometimes violently."[14]

At Amazon, team players are not defined as "people who go along with the group's consensus."[15] Instead, leaders are "obligated to respectfully challenge decisions when they disagree, even when doing so is uncomfortable or exhausting; they do not compromise for the sake of social cohesion."[16] (Our emphasis). People at Amazon tend to understand this obligation, not only to the company, but also to the customer and to the shareholder.

Many CEOs claim that they welcome different viewpoints. But unless you actually walk the talk, people will fear the "shooting the messenger" syndrome.

HAVE BACKBONE; DISAGREE AND COMMIT

While having every individual involved on board for key decisions is nice, there's a cost to having this as a policy: everyone can certainly recall countless experiences of postponed decision-making due to one or a few people's objections.

In most functionally organized companies, critical decisions are made by leaders through committees or through seeking consensus among the participants who are dedicated functional executives. These players rarely have an integrated picture of the customers, and as a result, instead of someone taking full ownership to decide, the group makes consensus-based decisions that usually inadequate in quality, slow in speed, and lacking in individual accountability.

Such a problem can be greatly exacerbated when decisions at hand have both innate uncertainty and pressing urgency. Nobody is a fortune teller, no one can be 100% sure regarding what will happen in three or five years down the road. How to solve the deadlock?

Bezos suggested the phrase "disagree and commit" as a heuristic way to save time. He notes that after all the facts have been considered and all views expressed, "if you have a conviction on a particular direction even though there's no consensus, it's helpful to say, 'Look, I know we disagree on this but will you gamble with me on it? Disagree and commit?' By the time you're at this point, no one can know the answer for sure, and you'll probably get a quick yes."[17]

This is not a one-way approach, but a two-way approach. Leaders can use this approach for high-velocity decision-making, and in fact should be prepared to practice this principle themselves. For example, when Bezos and the team had differing views regarding one particular Amazon Studios original, Bezos himself chose to greenlight it by following "disagree and commit." Staying consistent to his espoused principles in this case saved the group enormous time and resources.[18]

MINIMIZE REGRETS

When facing high-stakes destiny-defining decisions of enormous uncertainty, Bezos will resort to the ultimate weapon in his decision-making armor: the regret minimization framework.

He explained, "All of my best decisions in business and in life have been made with heart, intuition, guts and, you know, not analysis. When you can make a decision with analysis, you should do so, but it turns out in life that you most important decisions are always made with instinct, intuition, taste and heart . . . . When I'm 80, I want to have minimized the number of regrets that I have in my life. And most of our regrets are acts of omission, they're things we didn't try, it's the path untraveled. Those are the things that haunt us."[19] This is how Bezos made his destiny-defining decision twenty-five years ago when the Internet was still in its infancy: whether to continue his lucrative and promising Wall-Street career or to embark on an unknown adventure of starting his own business.

WHAT IF A DECISION GOES WRONG?

In his first shareholder letter in 1997, Bezos stated, "We will make bold rather than timid investment decisions where we see a sufficient probability of gaining market leadership advantages. Some of these investments will pay off, others will not, and we will have learned another valuable lesson in either case."

A wrong decision may not be career-ending in Amazon, but Bezos will make sure the lesson is well learnt.

So what's unique about Amazon's way of learning a lesson? The secret weapon is to consider inputs. People will be asked questions such as what factors should have been considered (and possibly weren't), what assumptions were made (and why some of them were unreasonable), what critical technological breakthrough was bet on (and why it did not happen as expected), and more.

Much more important than such post-mortem analysis is mid-course adjustment. Bezos said, "You need to be good at quickly recognizing and correcting bad decisions. If you're good at course correcting, being wrong may be less costly than you think, whereas being slow is going to be expensive for sure."[20]

SCALE UP GOOD DECISION-MAKING

In essence, decision-making is about making choices.

Without deliberate cultivation, everyone will have different answers based on his or her own preferences. That's natural.

However, for business-related issues, Bezos demands good decision-making from everyone at Amazon following the same principles and methodologies.

So here comes the billion-dollar question: how to scale high-velocity and high-quality decision-making?

CRYSTALIZE CONSISTENT PRINCIPLES

In his first Shareholder Letter, Bezos wrote: "Because of our emphasis on the long term, we may make decisions and weigh tradeoffs differently than some companies. Accordingly, we want to share with you our fundamental management and decision-making approach so that you, our shareholders, may confirm that it is consistent with your investment philosophy:

- We will continue to focus relentlessly on our customers.
- We will continue to make investment decisions in light of long-term market leadership considerations rather than short-

term profitability considerations or short-term Wall Street reactions.

- We will continue to measure our programs and the effectiveness of our investments analytically, to jettison those that do not provide acceptable returns, and to step up our investment in those that work best. We will continue to learn from both our successes and our failures.
- We will make bold rather than timid investment decisions where we see a sufficient probability of gaining market leadership advantages. Some of these investments will pay off, others will not, and we will have learned another valuable lesson in either case.
- When forced to choose between optimizing the appearance of our GAAP accounting and maximizing the present value of future cash flows, we'll take the cash flows.
- We will share our strategic thought processes with you when we make bold choices (to the extent competitive pressures allow), so that you may evaluate for yourselves whether we are making rational long-term leadership investments.
- We will work hard to spend wisely and maintain our lean culture. We understand the importance of continually reinforcing a cost-conscious culture, particularly in a business incurring net losses.
- We will balance our focus on growth with emphasis on long-term profitability and capital management. At this stage, we choose to prioritize growth because we believe that scale is central to achieving the potential of our business model.
- We will continue to focus on hiring and retaining versatile and talented employees, and continue to weight their compensation to stock options rather than cash. We know our success will be largely affected by our ability to attract and retain a motivated employee base, each of whom must think like, and therefore must actually be, an owner."[21]

It is hard to make good decisions and it is much harder to crystalize decision-making principles. Just imagine how much pain and efforts this calls for. Just try to name who else has done this. The list won't be long.

So why did Bezos choose to do this? Why did he choose to be this loud and clear, leaving himself no room for wavering in the future?

This unambiguous manifesto, specific, observable, and verifiable as it were, enabled shareholders to make informed investment decisions regarding Amazon. It also provided customers with the company's decision catechism, so that they would be more willing to build a trust-based long-term relationship with Amazon.

But most importantly, this transparent and widely shared set of principles is for all current and future Amazon employees: a set of crystal-clear guidelines so that every single one of them can understand the decision-making logic, and be able to make the right choice when duty calls.

SPECIFY CONSISTENT METHODOLOGY: NARRATIVES

June 9, 2004 witnessed a brilliant innovation in human management practices. It all started with an email from Bezos: No PowerPoint presentations from now on at S-team (Amazon's core executive team, including Bezos, and his direct reports and selective two-level-down executives). From that day on, Amazon started a crusade against bullet points, and embarked on a journey towards what came to be known as "Six-Page Narratives[22]" (sometimes two pages only).

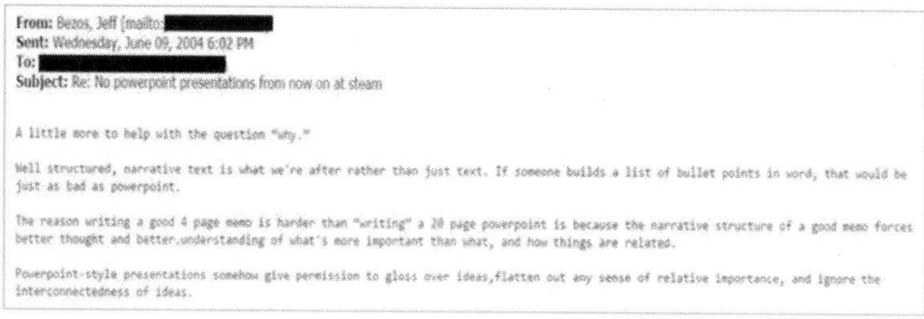

From: Bezos, Jeff [mailto:
Sent: Wednesday, June 09, 2004 6:02 PM
To:
Subject: Re: No powerpoint presentations from now on at steam

A little more to help with the question "why."

Well structured, narrative text is what we're after rather than just text. If someone builds a list of bullet points in word, that would be just as bad as powerpoint.

The reason writing a good 4 page memo is harder than "writing" a 20 page powerpoint is because the narrative structure of a good memo forces better thought and better.understanding of what's more important than what, and how things are related.

Powerpoint-style presentations somehow give permission to gloss over ideas,flatten out any sense of relative importance, and ignore the interconnectedness of ideas.

"A little more to help with the question "why."

Well structured, narrative text is what we're after rather than just text. If someone builds a list of bullet points in world, that would be just as bad as PowerPoint.

The reason writing a good 4-page memo is harder than "writing" a 20-page PowerPoint is because the narrative structure of a good memo forces better thought and better understanding of what's more important than what, and how things are related.

PowerPoint-style presentations somehow give permission to gloss over ideas, flatten out any sense of relative importance, and ignore the interconnectedness of ideas."

You may laugh at this idea, and seriously doubt the significance of this methodology, especially in the current era when PowerPoint has become virtually the second language of business. You are not alone. In some companies, there exists a standalone functional department whose only job is to produce PowerPoint presentations.

But Bezos was serious. This was not a capricious whim, but a well thought-through decision, particularly given the fact that the discussions and iterations required to produce a high-quality six-page memo might take a week or more. Bezos himself acknowledged that producing such documents was no small task: "Great memos are written and re-written, shared with colleagues who are asked to improve the work, set aside for a couple of days, and then edited again with a fresh mind. They simply can't be done in a day or two."[23]

Many people at Amazon vividly recall this practice even long after they left. John Rossman, a former Amazon executive, wrote, "I can't tell you how many of my weekends were consumed by this writing and editing process."[24]

So why was Bezos willing to make such a huge investment of people's time and effort? And why do people at Amazon revere this method so highly and regard it worthy of their days, nights, and weekends?

As Bezos noted in a 2012 interview with Charlie Rose, "When you have to write your ideas out in complete sentences and complete paragraphs, it forces a deeper clarity of thinking." This is quite a contrast with PowerPoint-style bullet points that give very little information. "This is easy for the presenter, but difficult for the audience," Bezos explained.

Writing the six-page narratives forces the author to conduct complete analysis, to distinguish between subtle nuances, to articulate the inner logic and set priorities for various ideas, and take full accountability for specific proposals. There is no wiggle room, no hiding place, and no safe haven. Everyone must put "skin in the game" and is to be held accountable for it.

Not only were newcomers to Amazon surprised to learn of this ban on PowerPoint, but they would also be shocked to learn that nearly every meeting at Amazon starts with attendees sitting in silence and reading the narratives for 15-30 minutes.

Why no presentation, just reading? Bezos said, "Executives are very good at interrupting . . . . The person will get halfway into their presentation and then some executive will interrupt the conversation and that question . . . . probably was going to be answered five slides in. So, if you read the whole six-page memo, it often happens to me, I get to page two and I have a question. I jot it in the margin and, by the time I get to page four, the question has been answered so I can just cross it off. It saves a lot of time.[25]" Reading memos together is a very effective way to ensure that everyone gets the full picture and is well-equipped for a high-quality discussion afterwards.

That's why, at Amazon, a meeting rarely ends without clear decisions or specific actions. Even those who missed the meeting can easily catch up regarding what and how a decision gets made.

Samir Lakhani, former Amazon employee, succinctly summed up the value of this practice succinctly by saying: "Bezos has given all employees a standard SOP (standard operating procedure) for ensuring the basics get done well."[26]

ENFORCE CONSISTENT APPROACH IN EVERY DECISION

As noted earlier, it is tough to make good decisions, and even tougher to crystalize decision-making principles. The toughest part is to walk the talks and consistently apply the stated principles when making every single decision.

In 2010, Bezos noted that "customers who browsed—but didn't buy—in the lubricant section of Amazon's sexual-wellness category were receiving personalized emails promoting a variety of gels and other intimacy facilitators."[27] He called a meeting to discuss this because he "believed the marketing department's e-mails caused customers embarrassment and should not have been sent."[28]

During the meeting, executives "argued that lubricants were available in grocery stores and drugstores and were not, technically, that embarrassing. They also pointed out that Amazon generated a significant volume of sales with such e-mails. Bezos didn't care; no amount of revenue was worth jeopardizing customer trust. It was a revealing—and confirming—moment. He (Bezos) was willing to slay a profitable aspect of his business rather than test Amazon's bond with its customers."[29]

It is exactly such defining moments that convince others what is important to you and how you will make decisions in tough situations. As Julie Weed wrote in the foreword of The Amazon Way, Amazon's "principles aren't slogans printed on wall posters and coffee mugs. They are lived and breathed every day by Amazonians from the CEO on down."

* * * * * * * *

Decision-making is about making choices. "In the end, we are our choices."[30]

The really tough choices are usually not the ones between right or wrong, better or worse, but the ones between two rational and reasonable options. Different people will make their different choices based on their different values, principles and preferences.

As a company, to ensure concerted and consistent choices throughout the organization, you need to crystalize your own principles and build a corresponding corporate culture to reinforce them.

No one will deny the importance of the right culture. The real problem is how to define it and how to build it. So what's the Amazon way? Let's proceed to the next chapter: Forever-Day-1 Culture.

REFLECTIONS AND IDEAS TO CONSIDER FOR YOUR COMPANY

CHAPTER HIGHLIGHTS

BUILDING BLOCK 6: FOREVER-DAY-1 CULTURE

Amazon, as an organization, is committed to be forever day 1, that is to combine the size and scale advantages of a big company, the speed and agility of a startup, and the continuous upgrade of organizational capabilities.

WHY DAY 1?

Day 2 is not an option
The divine discontent

HOW TO FEND OFF DAY 2?

The starter pack
Fight complacency
Kill bureaucracy
Own dependency

HOW TO BUILD A FOREVER-DAY-1 CULTURE?

Operationalize the culture
Create forcing mechanisms
Live and breathe them yourself
Invent memorable symbols and rewards

BUILDING BLOCK 6:

FOREVER-DAY-1 CULTURE

From the day he launched his new venture, Jeff Bezos has been obsessed with customers. Throughout the history of Amazon, this relentless focus has informed every decision and appeared in virtually every communication or action. In everything from the empty seat at early meetings (to represent the customer) to the recurring theme in every annual letter, customers are the guiding light for Amazon.

Do you know what else Bezos has been obsessed with? Organization. Whether at Amazon headquarter or fulfillment center, he always keeps an eye out for "flaws in the company's systems or even its corporate culture[1]".

So what kind of organization did Bezos want to build when he started this exciting adventure called Amazon?

If you read through all the shareholder letters that Bezos meticulously wrote over the past 22 years (1997-2018), the phrase "Day 1" appeared an amazing 22 times, with striking consistency. For the past 10 years, every shareholder letter has ended with the same line:

> *"As always, I attach a copy of our original 1997 letter. Our approach remains the same, and it's still Day 1." (2009-2015, with a one-word deviation in 2014[2])*

"As always, I attach a copy of our original 1997 letter. It remains Day 1." (2016-2018)

If you go to Amazon headquarters, you will find a building named "Day 1" where Bezos' office is located. Actually when he moved buildings, he took the name with him. The plate reads:

"There's so much stuff that has yet to be invented.
There's so much new that's going to happen."

Why is Day 1 so important to Bezos? Why has he felt such a strong urge to constantly remind everyone that it's still Day 1?

WHY DAY 1?

At the early stage of any start-up, the founder (or the small founding team) runs everything, from design to production, to sales, to delivery, and to book keeping. If luck is on their side, the business will soon outgrow the capacity of the founding team, and they will need to expand the team and build an organization.

Normally, in the beginning, the organization will still function with speed, nimbleness, and a risk-acceptance mentality, but as the business grows bigger, complexity starts increasing, and layers begin creeping in, the once-nimble start-ups inevitably fall into the trap of so called "large organizations" characterized by slowness, rigidity, and risk aversion.

Bezos graduated from Princeton University in 1986 with degrees in electrical engineering and computer science and initially intended to study physics. That's why he borrowed the term "entropy," an indicator of system's disorder and an idea that is of critical importance to thermodynamics.

In thermodynamics, entropy is a measure of the unavailable energy in a closed thermodynamic system that is also usually considered to be a measure of the system's disorder. This is a property of the system's state, which varies directly with any reversible change in heat in the system and inversely with the temperature of the system. The second law of thermodynamics states that for a thermodynamically defined process to actually occur, the sum of the entropies of the participating bodies must increase.

In short, in the world of physics, the total entropy, or level of disorder, of the universe is continually increasing. In the world of business, the inevitable path of any organization, if left unattended, will lead to decrease in efficiency and vitality, and increase in complexity and rigidity. This is the law of "entropy increase." In a way, it is a depressing law because it states that, no matter how great a company is now, without deliberate vigilance and institutional determination to fight entropy, it will fall into mediocrity.

Bezos' goal is to defy the law of entropy increase at Amazon, the company he builds. He declared that "We want to fight entropy. The bar has to continuously go up."[3]

DAY 2 IS NOT AN OPTION

Entropy may make a lot of sense to a physics or science major, but how to explain this abstract concept in layman's terms so that everyone at Amazon could understand it and embrace it?

Bezos' evocative and sticky model of "Day 1 vs. Day 2" has proved to be an immediate and useful way. This simple phrase captured Bezos' aspiration for Amazon to grow aggressively in scale and scope while preserving the entrepreneurial vitality of a startup, and building on the numerous advantages of a large company at the same time.

To defy the law of entropy increase is, by default, never easy. Bezos was fully aware of the challenge. As he noted, "There are some subtle traps that even high-performing large organizations can fall into as a matter of course, and we'll have to learn as an institution how to guard against them."[4]

So what does Day 2 look like in Bezos' mind? "Day 2 is stasis. Followed by irrelevance. Followed by excruciating, painful decline. Followed by death. And that is why it is always Day 1."[5]

To Bezos, someone who wanted to win so badly during childhood that he would cry publicly over the loss of a football game, Day 2 is never an option.

THE DIVINE DISCONTENT

As elaborated in "Building Block 4: Ground-Breaking Invention Machine," one of the many reasons why Bezos loves customers is their divine discontent. Their expectation always goes up.

Famous for his unreasonably high standards, Bezos is never satisfied with just meeting customers' expectations. What he always wants is to constantly delight them, to invent on their behalf, and to "wow" them. What he so adamantly wants to build is not just an invention machine, but one that continuously accelerates, because this is the only way to always stay ahead of customers' ever-rising expectations.

Customer obsession and Day 1 thinking are inextricably linked twin drivers of the Amazon management system. Amazon has to improve continuously in everything it does, in everyone it has, and with accelerating speed and agility.

In short, it's always Day 1, no matter how big Amazon gets in size.

HOW TO FEND OFF DAY 2?

There is no simple answer to this age-old problem that has been a source of trouble for almost every organization on the planet. There are many culprits and many traps that can lead to Day 2; some obvious, but some much more subtle and deeply imbedded in human nature. So, where to start?

THE STARTER PACK

Bezos identified this challenge early on, and has put a great deal of thinking into finding a solution. In his 2016 Shareholder Letter, he offered a starter pack of essentials for Day 1 defense. It includes:

- True customer obsession
- Resist proxies
- Embrace external trends
- High-velocity decision making

TRUE CUSTOMER OBSESSION

For Amazon, customer obsession is the first principle. For Bezos, it is essential to the Day 1 vitality. Why? It crystalizes the core purpose of the enterprise into something that drives behavior and decisions forever. People who are committed to delighting divinely discontent customers, beautifully so and wonderfully so, will be driven to continuously improve, innovate and invent on their behalf, and to make sure that organizational capability will rise faster than the ever-rising customer expectations.

They will become relentless in personal growth, in organizational capacity-building and in the continual endeavor to "experiment patiently, accept failures, plant seeds, protect saplings, and double down when you see customer delight. A customer-obsessed culture best creates the conditions where all of that can happen."[6]

RESIST PROXIES

Bezos said, "As companies get larger and more complex, there's a tendency to manage to proxies. This comes in many shapes and sizes, and it's dangerous, subtle, and very Day 2. A common example is process as proxy."[7]

Processes are a means to an end, initially designed to make business operation more scalable. However, as a company grows bigger, processes actually can become an end by themselves, so complicated that most people don't know how to navigate through them and in some cases, customer service is compromised to serve requirements of the internal processes, and focus on inputs, outputs and their linkage gets lost.

EMBRACE EXTERNAL TRENDS

Most Day 2 companies lack the necessary vigilance to respond to key external changes. They are slow in detecting the early warning signals, slow in assessing the possible impact on existing business and new opportunities, and slow in making decisions to adjust resource allocation or team assignment to confront these new realities.

Actually, many behave as if the world is still spinning based on the existing order and they can still prolong the past glories. Consciously or not, they resist the new trends rather than embrace them.

When faced with new digital technologies, such as big data, machine learning, and artificial intelligence, Day 2 companies question how realistic it is to apply new technologies to existing business: how much real impact the enormous investments required could indeed have on the business and what would be the return on investment.

Since the innate uncertainty of technology and future business development limits the possibility of nailing down a specific number of expected returns with bullet-proof accuracy, such discussions usually end nowhere.

This provides those Day 2 leaders clinging to the past with an opportunity to avoid such thinking about the future; they continue their happy life within a cocoon of static illusion.

HIGH-VELOCITY DECISION MAKING

As we have fully explored in the previous chapter, Amazon challenges the common trap of applying a "one-size-fits-all" heavy-weight approach to most decisions, including those changeable, reversible Type 2 decisions.

Indeed not every decision needs to go all the way to the top, to wait for all the information, and to require lengthy approvals and the agreement of all.

The cumulative effect of these practices is to engrain a daily culture of setting ambitious, aspirational yet well-thought-through goals combined with a clearly defined set of metrics to monitor and learn from these experiments in order to continuously improve.

So other than factors mentioned in Bezos' starter pack, what else could drag an organization into Day 2? There is no rocket science here. The usual suspects are complacency, bureaucracy, and interdependency that blurs the lines of accountability.

FIGHT COMPLACENCY

The fact that Bezos loves customers for their "divine discontent" reveals something both subtle and crucial about him. Bezos is a man of divine discontent himself and his insights about customers also perfectly apply to himself. He constantly sets the bar higher than the most discontent of his customer.

In everything he chooses to do, Jeff Bezos aims for something bigger, better (not slightly better, but significantly better by magnitude), differentiated or totally new. His goal is not merely to match the best offering in the market, but to become the standard setter. He needs to win in a big way, and also in a way that makes him proud.

As a person, Bezos' relentless drive for continuous improvement is hardwired in his DNA; as Amazon founder and CEO, he needs to inject this quality throughout the company as an explicitly stated value and operating principle.

What could be his archenemy in this mission? Complacency. "More than anything else, he (Bezos) fears and loathes complacency," says former Amazon executive John Rossman.

Bezos was truly concerned that as Amazon grew bigger and became more successful, complacency would replace "our spirit and our desire to take risks . . . . we would cease to insist on the highest standards and gradually entangle ourselves in a giant ball of red tape."[8] He explicitly told his executive team that if Amazon fell into this trap, the company would die.

There is no easy way to fight complacency, which usually creeps into any organization. Amazon tackles this organizational evil by relentlessly raising the bar. This remedy may seem too simple. Almost everyone knows it. But the real challenge here is the unyielding determination to enforce it throughout the entire organization.

At Amazon, people must think about how to improve continuously. They must tackle challenges such as: for the same thing, how to get it done with less; for continuing to delight and wow customers, what new things are to be done.

KILL BUREAUCRACY

As explained in "Building Block 2: Continuous Bar-Raising Talent Pool," Bezos hates bureaucracy. For him, this is personal and probably inherited from his grandpa, a real builder.

Bezos is not alone in this front. This is a common disgust shared by A-players. For any organization entrenched in bureaucracy, the A-players will quit, just as Bezos' grandpa did.

Then there are lovers of bureaucracy, the C- and D-players. They can hide behind the bullet-proof shield of bureaucracy, and protect themselves from transparency, accountability, or measurability. Without extreme caution and continuous nipping in the bud, bureaucracy can quickly encroach upon your entire organization, drive away top performers and, before you know it, get you onboard the one-way express to Day 2.

How to kill bureaucracy? Bezos has poured enormous thought into this aspect. Three practices for your consideration.

BUDGET CONTROL

Amazon is probably the least desirable place to go for anyone interested in empire-building, because there is simply no money for it. Amazon has become notoriously famous for its low-cost operation, which is designed to squeeze out bureaucracy.

INDIRECT HEADCOUNTS

Amazon regards those who are directly involved in the creation of new skills or better customer experiences as direct headcounts. All others are indirect headcounts. The company has always maintained stringent control over indirect headcounts. Bezos is particularly vigilant in eschewing middle management, as he believes bureaucracy-loving C- and D-players usually reside there. This is probably one of the key contributors for Amazon's impressively low G&A expenses: only 1.5% as of total revenue.

SIMPLIFY PROCESSES

Bezos fully recognizes the value of good process. Without defined process, business can't scale. Then how to distinguish bureaucracy from good process? Here is a checklist of warnings[9] by former Amazon executive John Rossman:

- When the rules can't be explained;
- When they don't favor the customer;
- When you can't get redress from a higher authority
- When you can't get an answer to a reasonable question
- When there is no service-level agreement or guaranteed response time built into the process
- When the rules simply don't make sense

If any of the above-described situations occur, you need to re-examine and simplify the processes. Good processes must deliver right outputs, display right inputs at each step, and must be designed for fewer handoffs, better transparency, and more integration of decision-making and clear end-to-end accountability.

OWN DEPENDENCY

There is a particular pain that every founder or business leader has to endure at some point: when people or teams fail to achieve a certain goal, fingers will be pointed and accusations made.

How to cut through this seemingly inevitable internal dependency and, once and for all, put an end to this endless war of finger-pointing?

Most companies would follow traditional practices, such as KPI, group-based incentives, and other mechanisms to encourage cross-division collaboration.

Bezos, always seeking better or unconventional ideas, will not settle for these commonly-adopted but proven-ineffective approaches. He finally cracked this especially hard-to-solve problem in 2003 with a three-step methodology:

1. *"Whenever possible, take over the dependencies so you don't have to rely on someone else.*

2. *If that is impossible, negotiate and manage unambiguous and clear commitments from others.*
3. *Create hedges wherever possible. For every dependency, devise a fallback plan."*[10]

Such an ambitious approach requires an operational discipline for consistent, successful execution. Making sure every dependency functions well and can deliver on time, on budget and up to the specific and challenging standards required, is a daunting challenge. It takes an ultimate sense of true ownership of everyone to pull it off. Without the right people and the right data and metrics system, it won't happen.

Incidentally, Bezos' seemingly unorthodox approach to manage internal dependency put Amazon onto the journey to discover AWS.

HOW TO BUILD A FOREVER-DAY-1 CULTURE?

To build a Forever-Day-1 organization, you need a corresponding corporate culture that reinforces the continued growth of this quality. Once established, like it or not, culture tends to become so rooted in the organization psyche, or so hardwired in the organization DNA, that it will be long, lasting and very hard to change. No one will deny the importance of the right culture. The real problem is how to define it and how to build it.

OPERATIONALIZE THE CULTURE

How to define a company's culture? As Bezos explained, "You can write down your corporate culture, but when you do so, you're discovering it, uncovering it – not creating it."[11]

Culture is normally created during the entire life span of an organization, with the strongest foundation laid in the beginning by its founding members. Their day-to-day behavior, their decision-making principles, their choices on people selection, promotion and hire and fire, their enforcement of key principles, and their past success and failure are the essential shaping forces.

Amazon's mission is "We strive to offer our customers the lowest possible prices, the best available selection, and the utmost convenience." Amazon's vision is "To be Earth's most customer-centric company, where customers can find and discover anything they might want to buy online."

Amazon's Leadership Principles have evolved over the years. Back in 1998, Amazon only had five values: "customer obsession, frugality, bias for action, ownership and high bar for talent,"[12] very different from most traditional companies. It later added innovation. Today, Amazon uses a set of 14 Leadership Principles to define its corporate culture. This is defined by the Amazon leadership team, not by Bezos alone.

1. Customer Obsession
2. Ownership
3. Invent and Simplify
4. Are Right, A Lot
5. Learn and Be Curious
6. Hire and Develop the Best
7. Insist on the Highest Standards
8. Think Big
9. Bias for Action
10. Frugality
11. Earn Trust
12. Dive Deep
13. Have Backbone; Disagree and Commit
14. Deliver Results

With slight variations (Invent and Simplify instead of innovation, and Hire and Develop the Best instead of high bar for talent), the original values have been inherited and enriched.

What makes Amazon unique is that it didn't stop at crafting abstract concepts, as many companies do. That's one of the key reasons why cultures in most organizations have been reduced to lofty slogans and inspirational wall hangings.

For each leadership principle, Amazon specifies the expected behavior. For example, what does "Customer Obsession" really mean?

> *Leaders start with the customer and work backwards. They work vigorously to earn and keep customer trust. Although leaders pay attention to competitors, they obsess over customers.*[13]

And what does "Insist on the Highest Standards" really mean?

> *Leaders have relentlessly high standards – many people may think these standards are unreasonably high. Leaders are continually raising the bar and driving their teams to deliver high-quality products, services, and processes. Leaders ensure that defects do not get sent down the line and that problems are fixed so that they stay fixed.*[14]

These 2-3 sentences are of pivotal importance in what sets Amazon apart from others.

Why? Because without this kind of detailed description, principles are abstract terms way up in the sky, lofty but impractical. Once you bring them down to clear and specific behaviors on the ground, they become operational, and everyone and anyone can start practicing them accordingly.

More subtly, clear and specific descriptions transform abstract ideals such as culture, value and principles, into guidelines that are observable, verifiable, and measurable.

While it's difficult to judge whether someone is truly customer obsessed or not; we can always tell whether this person actually starts with the customer and works backwards, or whether he constantly fixates on the competitor or he habitually starts from existing competency. When there is a conflict, does he work vigorously to earn and keep customer trust, or prioritize short-term money-making or his personal and department performance?

It's also difficult to judge whether someone insists on the highest standards or not. How to measure "high" and "highest"? The three-sentence explanations offer clear guidance. Are this person's standards regarded as unreasonably high by many? Is he continually raising the bar, or fairly satisfied with the status quo? When defects pop up, can he get to the root causes and eradicate the bugs for good, or does he just put on a Band-Aid as a temporary patch, and the same or similar problems will emerge later?

By now, you probably start to appreciate the beauty of the clear and specific behavioral descriptions after each leadership principle. This is what we call operationalizing the culture.

We strongly recommend that you read the complete set of Amazon 14 Leadership Principles in the appendix of this book. It will be well worth your time. While reading, you may think which ones could work for you, and which ones could enhance your business and organization.

CREATE FORCING MECHANISMS

So how can you ensure that your leadership principles will be consistently executed as your enterprise grows? One effective approach used at Amazon is the forcing mechanisms.

Start by making a list of the core values, cultures or principles you would like to reinforce in the organization and operationalize each item by providing clear and specific behavioral description. Many companies have probably done this part already, and found that the frustrating aspect of values, cultures or principles is that they are easier to state than to live. How to enforce them is the real challenge.

Amazon has created a system of simple but effective forcing mechanisms to ensure that everyone in the organization really lives and breathes the stated values and principles. Let's take Amazon's favorite and perennial number one principle, Customer Obsession, as an example.

WEEKLY CHECK-IN

Every week, Bezos asks his executives the same question: what can we do better for the customers. He asks this every week. No exception.

EMPTY CHAIR

In the early days of Amazon, Bezos would keep an empty chair in the room to constantly remind everyone that even if customers could not personally attend meetings, their interests should always be considered and fully represented.

PRESS RELEASE

As mentioned in "Building Block 4: Ground-Breaking Invention Machine," at Amazon, every project team responsible for new product or service development is required to create a press release, defining the target customers and describing the perceived benefits and highlights from the customers' perspective.

CALL-CENTER TRAINING

Each year, some managers are required to participate in a two-day training session at a call-center. This direct interaction with customers is designed to help them gain a first-hand understanding of customers' frustrations and pain points, and also to provide them with the precious humility to recognize that despite its widely applauded success, Amazon still needs to continuously improve.

FEEDBACK TRACKING

Given that in the digital age, a seemingly random post can go viral in no time, and if not handled properly in time, the damage from a negative post could be disastrous, Amazon has invested millions to build a system to systematically track customer feedback in real time.

THE ANDON CORD

At Amazon, if the customer care team constantly receives similar customer complaints about one product, they are fully authorized to pull the Andon Cord: to temporarily remove the product from the website.

This practice, adopted from the Toyota Production System, is to empower frontline people (in this case the service agents) to immediately remove from the website any product reported to have defects. The product page can only be restored after the source of the defect had been identified and corrected.

Of course the removal will hurt the retail team's performance in the short-term, but Bezos whole-heartedly supports this mechanism. "If you retail guys can't get it right, you deserve to be punished,"[15] he said.

AUTOMATED REFUND

If a service or product provided is discovered to be subpar, instead of waiting for customer complaints posted online or communicated via the call center, Amazon can detect the glitch and take the initiative to refund customers via its automated systems.

HOW DOES THIS WORK?

"We build automated systems that look for occasions when we've provided a customer experience that isn't up to our standards, and those systems then proactively refund customers. One industry observer recently received an automated email from us that said, 'We noticed that you experienced poor video playback while watching the following rental on Amazon Video On Demand: Casablanca. We're sorry for the inconvenience and have issued you a refund for the following amount: $2.99. We hope to see you again soon.' Surprised by the proactive refund, he ended up writing about the experience: Amazon 'noticed that I experienced poor video playback . . . .' And they decided to give me a refund because of that? Wow . . . . Talk about putting customers first."[16]

LIVE AND BREATHE THEM YOURSELF

In addition to the designs mentioned above to guide the organization daily, the most powerful forcing mechanism has to do with personally modelling the behavior expected from everyone.

On this front, Bezos is really a man of his word. His personal and persistence passion for prioritizing customers' interests to meet and exceed his own unreasonably high standards has tremendously shaped Amazon DNA and elevated Amazon's "customer obsession" to a whole new level.

There are numerous anecdotes about how adamant Bezos could become on issues that affect customers. Here are two examples.

PRICING

As we all know, Everyday Low Price is one of Walmart's secret weapons. Bezos not only learned it from Walmart, but also upgraded it in the digital context. At Amazon, it is the pricing bots that crawl websites, collect competitors' prices, and automatically adjust Amazon's pricing, enabling Amazon to always match the lowest prices.

An Amazon executive once asked Bezos whether Amazon should continue to enforce the matching price policy when the retailer with the lowest-price offering was actually out of stock. The logic is persuasive: why cut your margin when there is no real need to do so?

Bezos immediately rejected the suggestion. He said that doing so would force customers to grudgingly accept the higher price this time, but the bad feeling associated with Amazon for doing so would last a lot longer. His devotion to what customers would think and feel about this issue speaks volumes about his values.

What Bezos did is a great example of how a leader at Amazon should behave: work vigorously to earn and keep customer trust, as specified in the Leadership Principles.

This is the same underlying reason why AWS launched "AWS Trusted Advisor" in 2012, a service that monitors customer usage, and offers advise on how to improve performance, enhance security, and save money. Indeed, Amazon would proactively inform customers of possible savings.

Bezos said it best, "**Our pricing objective is to earn customer trust**, not to optimize short-term profit dollars."[17] (Our emphasis).

QUESTION MARK

Amazon has an official system to rank the severity of an internal emergency. It goes from a low of Sev-5 to a high of Sev-1. However, there is a severity level that trumps everything: an email directly from Bezos with his famous "question mark."

Bezos published his email address and welcomed customers to write directly to him regarding any issues they encountered along the way. Whenever a certain issue caught his attention, he would add a question mark on the message and forward it to the relevant person(s) at Amazon.

Whenever anyone receives a question mark message from Bezos, he or she is expected to drop everything, immediately get to the bottom of the issue and come up with a solution that would permanently solve this issue. A thorough analysis of why the issue happened in the first place and how to fix it so that such problem would stay fixed (never to recur) had to be presented to Bezos himself.

This is "Bezos' way to ensure that potential problems are addressed and that the customer's voice is always heard inside Amazon."[18]

THE PINK IPOD

One year Amazon ordered 4,000 pink iPods from Apple for Christmas. However, in mid-November Apple informed Amazon to expect a delay in delivery.

If you were the person in charge, how would you react to this bad news? The common practice would be to notify customers of the expected delay in their order, and apologize, while specifying that this disappointment was not our fault and there was nothing we could do about it. Polite and professional. What a perfect solution.

This is indeed the default solution for many companies around the globe. But at Amazon, for those who are truly obsessed with customers and who are truly committed to doing whatever humanly possible to delight customers, this was not the answer.

Instead, the Amazon team in charge went out and bought 4,000 pink iPods on the market, hand-sorted them, and ensured in-time shipment to customers.

From a financial perspective, it made no sense, but Bezos gave the team full support and total approval without any question or any hesitation. This was the right thing to do according to the Amazon Leadership Principles, and this is exactly the right kind of behavior that Bezos would like to see at Amazon.

INVENT MEMORABLE SYMBOLS AND REWARDS

How to make values, cultures and principles memorable? How to reward people who demonstrate full embodiment of the core elements? Again Amazon has flared his relentless drive to invent in shaping an organization.

10,000 YEAR CLOCK

Bezos personally invested in the building a 10,000 Year Clock of "monumental scale" inside the mountains of West Texas. As he put it:

> *"It's a special Clock, designed to be a symbol, an icon for long-term thinking.... a Clock that ticks once a year, where the century hand advances once every 100 years, and the cuckoo comes out on the millennium. As I see it, humans are now technologically advanced enough that we can create not only extraordinary wonders but also civilization-scale problems. We're likely to need more long-term thinking.*[19]"

JUST DO IT AWARD

To reinforce the leadership values called Bias for Action, Bezos instituted the "Just Do It Award". What's unique about this award is the prize. Given his constant reinforcement of frugality, Bezos came up with the totally unorthodox idea of having old sneakers, worn and torn, mounted and bronzed. Interestingly enough, this prize is highly coveted. Winners usually visibly and proudly display their prize in their offices.

DOOR DESK AWARD

At Amazon, the door desk is a symbol of enduring frugality. It reminds every one of the early days when Bezos used doors for desktops. The Door Desk Award rewards people who have "a well-built idea that helps us to deliver lower prices to customers" and the prize is a door desk ornament.[20]

As with everything that Bezos is committed to, his search for powerful symbols is also relentless. In Amazon's 2009 annual shareholder meeting, Bezos made "light bulbs" his new symbol for ultimate frugality. He said, "Every vending machine has light bulbs in it to make the advertisement more attractive . . . . so they went around to all of our fulfillment centers and took all the light bulbs out."

The estimated savings on electricity costs was merely tens of thousands of dollars. Not a big thing by itself. But the message was so loud and clear that everyone, employees and shareholders, got a very specific sense of what frugality means and, more importantly, what the standards of frugality are at Amazon.

* * * * * * * * *

By now, you should have a holistic view about all the six building blocks of the Amazon management system. It may occur to you that the Forever-Day-1 culture is both a result and an enabler of what Amazon has achieved for the past 25 years.

It has been the North Star from Day 1 that constantly keeps Amazon in conceiving a Customer-Obsessed Business Model (Building Block 1), cultivating a Continuous Bar-Raising Talent Pool (Building Block 2), constructing an AI-Powered Data and Metrics System (Building Block 3), creating a Ground-Breaking Invention Machine (Building Block 4) and constituting a mechanism for High-Velocity and High-Quality Decision-Making (Building Block 5).

It encourages, or in many ways, urges people at Amazon to continuously challenge the status quo for better and more, to ceaselessly seek new ideas, big and unique, to relentlessly invent, experiment, start over, rinse and repeat again and again. No matter how small the initial seed is, such undying Day-1 spirit will make it big. All these endeavors will in turn reinforce the conviction in the Forever-Day-1 culture.

As with everything else deliberately designed by Bezos, the Amazon Management System is also a self-reinforcing flywheel.

REFLECTIONS AND IDEAS TO CONSIDER FOR YOUR COMPANY

CHECKLIST OF THE AMAZON MANAGEMENT SYSTEM

	Building Blocks	The Amazon Way
1	Customer-Obsessed Business Model	Online and offline platform, ecosystem, and infrastruct provider Central idea based on customer obsession, inventing fo the customers, long-term thinking and cash generatio over earnings
2	Continuous Bar-Raising Talent Pool	Definition: builder, owner and mental toughness Recruiting: bar raiser, rigorous process and self-selective mechanism Motivating: builder's dreamland, young man's paradise and the high standards
3	AI-Powered Data and Metrics System	Single source of truth Metrics: ultra-detailed, end-to-end, real-time, tracking inputs and need to be verified and be assigned to specific metric owner Powerful AI-powered tools able to automate decision-making
4	Ground-Breaking Invention Machine	Relentless drive to invent: daring to learn new skills, to kill own business, to fail, in a big way Seek and build big ideas continuously (the press release), and construct cross-functional full-time and co-located two-pizza team with the right project leader
5	High-Velocity and High-Quality Decision-Making	Two types of decision-making: type 1 (one-way doors) and type 2 (two-way doors). For type 2 decisions, speed matters. Let the metrics owner make the call. If approval required, one level only. For type 1 decisions, focus on a few. Find out the best truth, imagine the possible change, combat group thinking, and if facing disagreement, disagree and commit. To scale up good decision-making, need to crystalize consistent principles and methodologies (the six-page narratives) and enforce them in every decision.
6	Forever-Day-1 Culture	To fend off Day 2: true customer obsession, resist proxies, embrace external trends, high-velocity decision-making, fight complacency, kill bureaucracy, and own dependency To build a forever-Day-1 culture: operationalize by observable behaviors, create forcing mechanisms, live and breathe them yourself, and invent memorable symbols and rewards.

TO LEADERS IN THE DIGITAL AGE

We hope you enjoyed reading this book and you are committed to embark on your own digital journey.

You have probably heard snippets of the Amazon story pieces here and there. Most of these should be correct, some exaggerated, and, some, once out of context, could be very misleading. That's why we've devoted so much time and energy to verifying the facts, connecting the dots, demystifying the urban legends, and putting everything into a systematic and holistic package.

Unlike the century-old way of business management designed for command and control, the Amazon Management System is designed for speed, agility, and scale. It has been proven to be a winning formula to survive and thrive in the digital age, a new era characterized by changes of unprecedented speed and magnitude.

We are not here to advocate a blind replication of all and everything in the Amazon Management System. Because we know only too well, from lessons learned through decades of consulting practice, that what really matters is the fit.

Why does the Amazon Management System work so well for Amazon? Because it best fits the personal values, principles, characters and styles of Jeff Bezos, Amazon's founder and CEO, and his core team; it also best fits the nature of Amazon's platform and infrastructure business.

What works for you? What fits you and your business best? No one has the perfect answer. You will have to experiment, iterate and invent your own.

You are not alone in this adventure. Let's explore together.

Always remember: it is still Day 1.

Ram and Julia
August 2, 2019

APPENDIX 1:

AMAZON 9-POINT MANAGEMENT AND DECISION-MAKING APPROACH

Excerpt from Bezos 1997 Shareholder Letter

Because of our emphasis on the long term, we may make decisions and weigh tradeoffs differently than some companies. Accordingly, we want to share with you our fundamental management and decision-making approach so that you, our shareholders, may confirm that it is consistent with your investment philosophy:

- We will continue to focus relentlessly on our customers.
- We will continue to make investment decisions in light of long-term market leadership considerations rather than short-term profitability considerations or short-term Wall Street reactions.
- We will continue to measure our programs and the effectiveness of our investments analytically, to jettison those that do not provide acceptable returns, and to step up our investment in those that work best. We will continue to learn from both our successes and our failures.

- We will make bold rather than timid investment decisions where we see a sufficient probability of gaining market leadership advantages. Some of these investments will pay off, others will not, and we will have learned another valuable lesson in either case.
- When forced to choose between optimizing the appearance of our GAAP accounting and maximizing the present value of future cash flows, we'll take the cash flows.
- We will share our strategic thought processes with you when we make bold choices (to the extent competitive pressures allow), so that you may evaluate for yourselves whether we are making rational long-term leadership investments.
- We will work hard to spend wisely and maintain our lean culture. We understand the importance of continually reinforcing a cost-conscious culture, particularly in a business incurring net losses.
- We will balance our focus on growth with emphasis on long-term profitability and capital management. At this stage, we choose to prioritize growth because we believe that scale is central to achieving the potential of our business model.
- We will continue to focus on hiring and retaining versatile and talented employees, and continue to weight their compensation to stock options rather than cash. We know our success will be largely affected by our ability to attract and retain a motivated employee base, each of whom must think like, and therefore must actually be, an owner.

APPENDIX 2:

AMAZON 14 LEADERSHIP PRINCIPLES

We use our Leadership Principles every day, whether we're discussing ideas for new projects or deciding on the best approach to solving a problem. It is just one of the things that makes Amazon peculiar.

1. CUSTOMER OBSESSION
   Leaders start with the customer and work backwards. They work vigorously to earn and keep customer trust. Although leaders pay attention to competitors, they obsess over customers.

2. OWNERSHIP
   Leaders are owners. They think long term and don't sacrifice long-term value for short-term results. They act on behalf of the entire company, beyond just their own team. They never say "that's not my job."

3. INVENT AND SIMPLIFY
   Leaders expect and require innovation and invention from their teams and always find ways to simplify. They are externally aware, look for new ideas from everywhere, and are not limited by "not

invented here." As we do new things, we accept that we may be misunderstood for long periods of time.

4. ARE RIGHT, A LOT

Leaders are right a lot. They have strong judgment and good instincts. They seek diverse perspectives and work to disconfirm their beliefs.

5. LEARN AND BE CURIOUS

Leaders are never done learning and always seek to improve themselves. They are curious about new possibilities and act to explore them.

6. HIRE AND DEVELOP THE BEST

Leaders raise the performance bar with every hire and promotion. They recognize exceptional talent, and willingly move them throughout the organization. Leaders develop leaders and take seriously their role in coaching others. We work on behalf of our people to invent mechanisms for development like Career Choice.

7. INSIST ON THE HIGHEST STANDARDS

Leaders have relentlessly high standards — many people may think these standards are unreasonably high. Leaders are continually raising the bar and drive their teams to deliver high quality products, services, and processes. Leaders ensure that defects do not get sent down the line and that problems are fixed so they stay fixed.

8. THINK BIG

Thinking small is a self-fulfilling prophecy. Leaders create and communicate a bold direction that inspires results. They think differently and look around corners for ways to serve customers.

9. BIAS FOR ACTION

Speed matters in business. Many decisions and actions are

reversible and do not need extensive study. We value calculated risk taking.

10. FRUGALITY

Accomplish more with less. Constraints breed resourcefulness, self-sufficiency, and invention. There are no extra points for growing headcount, budget size, or fixed expense.

11. EARN TRUST

Leaders listen attentively, speak candidly, and treat others respectfully. They are vocally self-critical, even when doing so is awkward or embarrassing. Leaders do not believe their or their team's body odor smells of perfume. They benchmark themselves and their teams against the best.

12. DIVE DEEP

Leaders operate at all levels, stay connected to the details, audit frequently, and are skeptical when metrics and anecdote differ. No task is beneath them.

13. HAVE BACKBONE; DISAGREE AND COMMIT

Leaders are obligated to respectfully challenge decisions when they disagree, even when doing so is uncomfortable or exhausting. Leaders have conviction and are tenacious. They do not compromise for the sake of social cohesion. Once a decision is determined, they commit wholly.

14. DELIVER RESULTS

Leaders focus on the key inputs for their business and deliver them with the right quality and in a timely fashion. Despite setbacks, they rise to the occasion and never settle.

ABOUT THE AUTHORS

Ram Charan's 27 books have sold over three million copies and include the *New York Times* bestseller *Execution*. He is a world-renowned business advisor, author and speaker who has spent the past 35 years working with many top companies, CEOs, and boards of our time. In his work with companies including GE, MeadWestvaco, Bank of America, DuPont, Novartis, EMC, 3M, Verizon, Aditya Birla Group, Tata Group, Max Group, and Grupo RBS, he is known for cutting through the complexity of running a business in today's fast changing environment to uncover the core business problem. His real-world solutions, shared with millions through his books and articles in top business publications, have been praised for being practical, relevant and highly actionable — the kind of advice you can use Monday morning.

Ram's introduction to business came early while working in the family shoe shop in a small town in northern India, where he was raised. When his talent for business was discovered, Ram was encouraged to develop it. He earned MBA and doctorate degrees from Harvard Business School, where he graduated with high distinction and was a Baker Scholar, then served on the faculties of Harvard Business School and Northwestern University before pursuing consulting full-time.

Ram's work takes him around the globe non-stop and gives him an unparalleled, up-to-date insider view of how economies and leading companies operate. Through keen observation and analysis, he forms powerful insights that help business leaders face their toughest challenges in the areas of growth, talent development, corporate governance, and profitability. His timely concrete advice is a powerful tool in navigating today's uncertain business climate. Former Chairman of GE Jack Welch says Ram "has the rare ability to distinguish meaningful from meaningless and transfer it in a quiet, effective way without destroying confidences," while Ivan Seidenberg, the former CEO of Verizon, calls Ram his "secret weapon."

Ram has coached more than a dozen leaders who went on to become CEOs. He reaches many more up-and-coming business leaders through in-house executive education programs. His energetic, interactive teaching style has won him several awards, including the Bell Ringer award at GE's famous Crotonville Institute and best teacher award at Northwestern. He was among *BusinessWeek's* top ten resources for in-house executive development programs

Ram has authored over 25 books since 1998 that have sold over 2 million copies in more than a dozen languages. Three of his books were *Wall Street Journal* bestsellers, including Execution, which he coauthored with former Honeywell CEO Larry Bossidy in 2002, which spent more than 150 weeks on the *New York Times* bestseller list. He also has written for publications including *Harvard Business Review, Fortune, BusinessWeek, Time, Chief Executive* and *USA TODAY.*

Ram was elected a Distinguished Fellow of the National Academy of Human Resources and has served on the Blue Ribbon Commission on Corporate Governance. He has served on the boards of Hindalco in India, Emaar, Austin Industries, Tyco Electronics, and Fischer and Porter. His newest book, *Amazon's Management System: The Ultimate Digital Business Engine That Creates Extraordinary Value for Both Customers and Shareholders,* is the first deep dive into the world's largest company designed to help everyone from established CEO's to fresh college grads by laying out the methodology and underpinnings of every decision that happens inside.

Julia Yang is a trusted advisor to entrepreneurs, founders, CEOs and executives, a reputation earned during nearly twenty years of relevant practice. She is currently working with Ram Charan to serve business leaders and explore new management practices in the digital age.

Prior to this, Julia was a consultant at McKinsey and a private equity investor at Bain Capital. She earned her MBA from Harvard Business School, along with master and bachelor degrees from Tsinghua University.

Julia also serves on the faculty of the joint MIT-Tsinghua MBA program, and on the board of Narada Foundation, a leading philanthropic organization.

NOTES

BUILDING BLOCK 1: CUSTOMER-OBSESSED BUSINESS MODEL

1 Brad Stone, The Everything Store, Little, Brown, and Company, 2013; Back Bay Books, 2014. New York.
2 Ibid.
3 Kristin Pryor, "A History of Amazon's Amazing Acquisitions," https://tech.co/news/history-amazon-acquisitions-2016-05.
4 Interviews with Amazon executives.
5 Interviews with Amazon executives.
6 Bezos 2018 Shareholder Letter.
7 Ibid.
8 Amazon 2018 Annual Report, https://ir.aboutamazon.com/annual-reports.
9 Bezos 2008 Shareholder Letter.
10 Bezos 1998 Shareholder Letter.
11 Bezos 2008 Shareholder Letter.
12 Bezos 2017 Shareholder Letter.
13 Bezos 2018 Shareholder Letter.
14 Bezos 2001 Shareholder Letter.
15 Bezos 1999 Shareholder Letter.
16 The law of diminishing returns is an economic principle stating that as investment in a particular area increases, the rate of profit from that investment, after a certain point, cannot continue to increase if other variables remain constant. As investment continues past that point, the return diminishes progressively. (https://searchcustomerexperience.techtarget.com/definition/law-of-diminishing-returns)
17 Bezos 2001 Shareholder Letter.
18 Amazon 2018 Annual Report, https://ir.aboutamazon.com/Capital IQ
19 Bezos 2017 Shareholder Letter.

BUILDING BLOCK 2: CONTINUOUS BAR-RAISING TALENT POOL

1 John Rossman, The Amazon Way, Clyde Hill Publishing, 2014.
2 Amazon Leadership Principles, https://www.amazon.jobs/en/principles.
3 Bezos 2003 Shareholder Letter.
4 John Rossman, The Amazon Way, Clyde Hill Publishing, 2014.
5 The Everything Store, Brad Stone, Little, Brown, and Company, 2013; Back Bay Books, 2014. New York.
6 Bezos 1997 Shareholder Letter.
7 Amazon 2010 Annual Report, https://ir.aboutamazon.com/annual-reports.
8 The Everything Store, Brad Stone, Little, Brown, and Company, 2013; Back Bay Books, 2014. New York.
9 Ibid.
10 Ibid.
11 bid.
12 Bezos 2017 Shareholder Letter.

BUILDING BLOCK 3: AI-POWERED DATA AND METRICS SYSTEM

1 Bezos said at the Yale Club in New York City in February, 2019.
2 W. Edwards Deming was a legendary business thinker and pioneer in quality control.
3 Interviews with Amazon execcutives, and The Amazon Way, John Rossman, 2014.
4 Bezos 2009 Shareholder Letter.
5 John Rossman, The Amazon Way, Clyde Hill Publishing, 2014.
6 Amazon 2002 Annual Report, https://ir.aboutamazon.com/annual-reports.
7 Bezos 2002 Shareholder Letter.
8 Brad Stone, The Everything Store, Little, Brown, and Company, 2013; Back Bay Books, 2014. New York.
9 Ibid,
10 Ibid.
11 Bezos 2018 Shareholder Letter.
12 Brad Stone, The Everything Store, Little, Brown, and Company, 2013; Back Bay Books, 2014. New York.
13 Bezos 2014 Shareholder Letter.

BUILDING BLOCK 4: GROUND-BREAKING INVENTION MACHINE

1 Chip Bayers, "The Inner Bezos," Wired, 1999, https://www.wired.com/1999/03/bezos-3/.
2 Bezos 2015 Shareholder Letter.
3 John Sviokla, "Innovation Lessons from Amazon", Harvard Business Review, 2008, https://hbr.org/2008/05/innovation-lessons-from-amazon.

4 Brad Stone, The Everything Store, Little, Brown, and Company, 2013; Back Bay Books, 2014. New York
5 Brad Stone, The Everything Store, Little, Brown, and Company, 2013; Back Bay Books, 2014. New York.
6 Bezos 2018 Shareholder Letter.
7 Bezos 2015 Shareholder Letter.
8 Collis, David, Andy Wu, Rembrand Koning, and Huaiyi CiCi Sun. "Walmart Inc. takes on Amazon.com." Harvard Business School Case 718-481, January 2018. (Revised May 2018.)
9 Bill Taylor, "How Coca-Cola, Netflix, and Amazon Learn from Failure," Harvard Business Review, 2017, https://hbr.org/2017/11/how-coca-cola-netflix-and-amazon-learn-from-failure.
10 Jeff Bezos, 2018 Shareholder Letter.
11 Jeff Bezos, 2018 Shareholder Letter.
12 Bill Taylor, "How Coca-Cola, Netflix, and Amazon Learn from Failure," HBR, 2017, https://hbr.org/2017/11/how-coca-cola-netflix-and-amazon-learn-from-failure.
13 Bezos interview with David Rubenstein at the Economic Club of Washington, D.C., 2018.
14 Interviews with Amazon executives.
15 Morgan Stanley Research, Dec. 6, 2018.
16 Bezos interview with David Rubenstein at the Economic Club of Washington, D.C., 2018.
17 Amazon 2018 Annual Report, https://ir.aboutamazon.com/annual-reports.
18 Interviews with Amazon executives.
19 Amazon 2018 Annual Report, https://ir.aboutamazon.com/annual-reports.
20 John Rossman, The Amazon Way, Clyde Hill Publishing, 2014.
21 Bezos 2017 Shareholder Letter.
22 John Rossman, The Amazon Way, Clyde Hill Publishing, 2014.
23 Bezos 2018 Shareholder Letter.
24 Bezos interview with Charlie Rose Show, 2012.
25 Bezos 2018 Shareholder Letter.
26 Bezos 2018 Shareholder Letter.
27 John Rossman, The Amazon Way, Clyde Hill Publishing, 2014.
28 Brad Stone, The Everything Store, Little, Brown, and Company, 2013; Back Bay Books, 2014. New York.
29 Amazon 2018 Annual Report, https://ir.aboutamazon.com/annual-reports.
30 Bezos 2010 Shareholder Letter.
31 Bezos 2011 Shareholder Letter.
32 Bezos 2014 Shareholder Letter.

BUILDING BLOCK 5: HIGH-VELOCITY AND HIGH-QUALITY DECISION MAKING

1 Bezos 2016 Shareholder Letter.
2 Bezos 2015 Shareholder Letter.
3 Bezos 2015 Shareholder Letter.

4 Bezos 2015 Shareholder Letter.
5 Bezos 2015 Shareholder Letter.
6 Ram Charan with Geri Willigan, The High-Potential Leader, Wiley, 2017, Hoboken, NJ.
7 Bezos 2016 Shareholder Letter.
8 Bezos interview with David Rubenstein at the Economic Club of Washington, D.C., 2018
9 http://www.feynman.com/science/the-challenger-disaster/
10 Daniel McGinn, "How Jeff Bezos Makes Decisions," Harvard Business Review, 2013, https://hbr.org/2013/10/how-jeff-bezos-makes-decisions.
11 Brad Stone, The Everything Store, Little, Brown, and Company, 2013; Back Bay Books, 2014. New York.
12 Brad Stone, The Everything Store, Little, Brown, and Company, 2013; Back Bay Books, 2014. New York.
13 Morgan Stanley Research, Dec. 6, 2018.
14 Brad Stone, The Everything Store, Little, Brown, and Company, 2013; Back Bay Books, 2014. New York.
15 Cass R. Sunstein, "Disagreement Results in Better Decision," HBR, 2015, https://hbr.org/2015/08/amazon-is-right-that-disagreement-results-in-better-decisions.
16 Amazon Leadership Principles.
17 Bezos 2016 Shareholder Letter.
18 Bezos 2016 Shareholder Letter.
19 Bezos interview with David Rubenstein at the Economic Club of Washington, D.C., 2018
20 Bezos 2016 Shareholder Letter.
21 Bezos 1997 Shareholder Letter.
22 Bezos 2017 Shareholder Letter.
23 Bezos 2017 Shareholder Letter.
24 John Rossman, The Amazon Way, Clyde Hill Publishing, 2014.
25 Bezos 2012 interview with Charlie Rose.
26 Samir Lakhani, "Things I liked about Amazon," Aug 27, 2017, https://medium.com/@samirlakhani/things-i-liked-about-amazon-4495ef06fbda.
27 Brad Stone, The Everything Store, Little, Brown, and Company, 2013; Back Bay Books, 2014. New York.
28 Ibid.
29 Ibid.
30 Bezos 2010 commencement speech at Princeton.

BUILDING BLOCK 6: FOREVER-DAY-1 CULTURE

1 Brad Stone, The Everything Store, Little, Brown, and Company, 2013; Back Bay Books, 2014. New York.
2 As always, I attach a copy of our original 1997 letter. Our approach remains the same, because it's still Day 1. (Bezos 2014 Shareholder Letter)
3 Bezos 1998 Shareholder Letter.
4 Bezos 2015 Shareholder Letter.
5 Bezos 2016 Shareholder Letter.

6 Bezos 2016 Shareholder Letter.
7 Bezos 2016 Shareholder Letter.
8 John Rossman, The Amazon Way, Clyde Hill Publishing, 2014.
9 Ibid.
10 Ibid.
11 Bezos 2015 Shareholder Letter.
12 Brad Stone, The Everything Store, Little, Brown, and Company, 2013; Back Bay Books, 2014. New York.
13 Amazon Leadership Principles.
14 Amazon Leadership Principles.
15 John Rossman, The Amazon Way, Clyde Hill Publishing, 2014.
16 Bezos 2013 Shareholder Letter.
17 Bezos 2008 Shareholder Letter.
18 Brad Stone, The Everything Store, Little, Brown, and Company, 2013; Back Bay Books, 2014. New York.
19 http://www.10000yearclock.net/learnmore.html
20 Brad Stone, The Everything Store, Little, Brown, and Company, 2013; Back Bay Books, 2014. New York.

INDEX